## Praise for *Feedforward Thinking*

"'What do you really want to achieve?' Mr. Hisano asked me this question when we first met. As I worked with Mr. Hisano, I became aware that I had been unconsciously stuck with my past bitter experiences and failures. By practicing *Feedforward Thinking*, my comfort zones have been updated one after another, and I have discovered the dreams that I truly want to fulfill. While I wish I had encountered Feedforward earlier in my life, I also think it might have been the best possible timing for me. I am convinced that this book will bring positive changes in the 'future world' you envision for yourself."

– YUSEI KIKUCHI, Major League Baseball Pitcher

"Hisano brilliantly flips the downsides of feedback into life-enhancing feedforward thinking, a holistic perspective each of us can use to enhance our lives as well as those around us."

– JOHN BERNARD, Nation's Leading Authority on Government Accountability, Author of *Government That Works*, Founder of AmericanStates.org

"Reversing time's arrow is a breakthrough intuition of Kazuyoshi Hisano. Instead of remaining prisoners within the boundaries of our past, Feedforward Thinking frees us to move into a successful life, switching our mindset from being past-oriented to being future-oriented. In the process we transform our brain into a good friend. *Feedforward Thinking* is not a WHAT-TO do book but rather a HOW-TO do book, full of real-life stories. In *Feedforward Thinking* Hisano shares his method built and tested during decades of hard work in the coaching field. We highly recommend *Feedforward Thinking* to individuals who believe that having a successful life is worthwhile, and to managers who wish to boost their leadership skills and their teams' performances"

– FEDERICO BORRA and GIORGIO TURCONI, Turbo Consulting, Italy

---

"Kayuyoshi Hisano has combined his extensive coaching and management experience with cognitive science, so he is ideally qualified to write on a concept that addresses a problem that many encounter; How to better identify the actions and routines that create the pathways toward achieving our goals, all this while unleashing the drive that sustains our focus and energy, in creating our future.

Hisano is right, there is a blockage, I have experienced this myself, a need to not only redirect our attention on how we identify the day-to-day steps that move us towards achieving our goal(s), but also to have a better understanding on how our brains work, particularly in mapping out the pathways towards our desired future. His solution is *Feedforward Thinking*.

In short, feedforward thinking provides an excellent concept and a central way of thinking for creating your future. This book outlines a step-by-step implementation of the concept with examples, and it is easy to follow. At the very least feedforward thinking will seamlessly compliment your current approach to achieving your goals, or it may indeed completely replace your existing framework. Most importantly though, you can start implementing today!"

– BRENTON LEITCH, Managing Director, Learning and Productivity, Australia

"Since I met Mr. Kazuyoshi Hisano back in 2020, I've learned from him how to use my brain's capacities to achieve my goals, either personal, family and/or business related, using his Gold Vision Method. Now, with this new book, Mr. Hisano, the Best CEO Coach of the World, did it again. *Feedforward Thinking* invites you to change your point of reference towards the future, hence, awakening the creative parts of your brain throughout your conversations. Used together, his Gold Vision Method (his previous book) and his Feedforward Thinking (this book), form a powerful operating system to achieve any goal, either personal or organizational, allow me to repeat that, ANY GOAL! What you will learn from this book is why feedback does not work to achieve our goals and how it takes us to get stuck in the past, as how our conversations can help us create our common future. So, do you want you and your team move from getting stuck towards achieving your goals? This is your book!"

– ALBERTO MOLINAR, CEO, Global Audit

---

"Norman Bodek has contributed greatly to the shifting of the prevailing paradigm from mass production to Lean and Agile by bringing out the genius of Japanese Gurus like Taiichi Ohno, Shigeo Shingo, Ryuji Fukuda and many others. He helped them to share their thought processes with the rest of the world. The last treasure that he fostered before he passed away in 2020 is Kazuyoshi Hisano.

Hisano's thoughts have the potential to shape the 21st century in the way Bodek's other 'discoveries' shaped the last century. In the Indian worldview, we live in the 'Kali Yuga', a period in which creative destruction is the best strategy. Information and 'intelligence' have been harnessed and learning from the past has been automated. The contribution we, as human beings, can bring is to 'materialize the future'.

Feedforward is a simple and powerful process to materialize the future. Feedforward Action (FFA), the structure that Sensei Hisano has developed, will be as fundamental as the P-D-C-A and should become a lesson that every individual can access and benefit from. The best investment one can make is to develop the capability to imagine and create the future.

The next generation has significantly different perspectives and values. Conditions have changed rapidly, and many managers find it difficult to deal with millennials. This book has very useful tips that can improve communication at all levels and will be especially useful for closing the 'generation gap'."

This is an important book, don't miss it."

– T.V. SURESH, TAO Consulting Systems

---

"Feedforward" may sound foreign as it differs from 'feedback' that most of us are familiar with. Feedforward serves as a key tool for individuals, businesses, and organizations to bring about growth and transformation. Distinguished from feedback, it is a friendly and powerful tool that encourages you to invite ideas from others and pull them into collaborative relations for advancement. I believe that this book, which is full of Mr. Hisano's insights, will greatly help you be a trustworthy leader in your field."

– DAVID DONGCHUL BAE, founder of Asia Future HR Institute, CEO at Startup Forum in Korea, leading businessman and strategist selected as "100 CEOs to Lead Asia for the Next Generation" by The Japan Times

---

"In this book, Hisano-san takes you on a journey through the concept of feedforward offering a refreshing perspective on personal and professional growth. Although I was familiar with the term from Boyd's OODA loop, its application in unlocking potential, as presented in this book, was an eye-opening revelation. The core idea of feedforward, focusing on the future rather than dwelling on past experiences, particularly resonated with me.

The most impactful aspect of feedforward, as explained in the book, is its ability to activate the prefrontal cortex, encouraging creative thinking and enhancing performance. This contrasts sharply with feedback, which often triggers the limbic system and can inhibit these functions. The neuroscience behind feedforward, especially how it increases dopamine in the prefrontal cortex, thus fostering motivation and cognitive flexibility, was both intriguing and convincing. This exploration into feedforward has fundamentally shifted my approach to problem-solving and goal-setting, emphasizing a forward-looking mindset."

– AHMED AVAIS, Business Agility Coach, Research Triangle Park, North Carolina

---

"HR departments across the globe encourage the management to give regular feedback to employees. But what good is the feedback to a person's success at work? Hisano sensei challenges this practice and what's more offers us a better way: 'feeding forward'. A book that must be read by anyone involved in management."

– NIHAT KARAOGLU - Tech Executive, Switzerland

---

# FEEDFORWARD
## THINKING

# FEEDFORWARD
# THINKING

Create The Future You Want

## KAZUYOSHI HISANO

PCS PRESS

Seattle, Washington

Publisher's Cataloging-in-Publication data

Names: Hisano, Kazuyoshi, author.
Title: Feedforward thinking : create the future you want / Kazuyoshi Hisano.
Description: Includes bibliographical references and index. | Seattle, WA: PCS Press, 2023.
Identifiers: LCCN: 2024930050 | ISBN: 979-8-9872585-4-5 (hardcover) | 979-8-9872585-3-8 (paperback) | 979-8-9872585-5-2 (ebook)
Subjects: LCSH Goal setting. | Self-actualization (Psychology). | Success. | Self-help. | BISAC SELF-HELP / General | SELF-HELP / Personal Growth / Success
Classification: LCC BF637.S8 .H57 2023| DDC 158--dc23

PCS Press
PCS Inc.
1420 5TH AVE, STE 4200
SEATTLE, WA 98101-2375
1-360-605-7508

Printed in the United States of America

Translated by Ellie Rie Shollenberger.
Edited by Bob Quinn, Laurie Regan, and George Trachilis.
Cover and book design by Bobbi Benson, Wild Ginger Press.

*To my wife Seiko Hisano
and my son Sho Hisano.*

# CONTENTS

# PROLOGUE

W hen you become conscious of your future and work toward it, you will see the desired results, and you will become happy. The *Feedforward Method* introduced in this book is easy to master for everyone. I have experienced the effect of feedforward myself.

More than 15 years ago, I met Dr. Hideto Tomabechi, who was an expert and authority in brain science. It indeed became a turning point in my life for me when I began learning from him the science of how to use the brain.

When one of my family members was diagnosed with a mental illness, I wanted to be of help, even if only a little. I read every medical book I could get my hands on, and I came to understand that understanding the brain seemed to be the key to the solution. While I was researching how I could learn about the brain, I came across Dr. Hideto Tomabechi, who is a world-famous cognitive scientist and known for his work in deprogramming the brainwashing of some leaders in the Aum cult group.

In my hope that if I learned from Dr. Tomabechi, it would help me help my family member, I became his apprentice. I started acquiring the knowledge of how the brain and mind work and the techniques to use them. I applied my learnings to this relative and observed that the illness was improving slowly but surely. My family member became healthy again by looking to the future.

---

When we think about the future and work toward it, we get desired results and become happy.

---

This concept above convinced me as I witnessed my family member's recovery from the illness. Soon after, I started applying this method to the team members in the company I was with then. It was not anything complicated. I simply met each team member monthly and asked, "What are you going to do next?" I encouraged the members to think about their future. Based on what they "wanted to do," I supported their decision-making for their future directions while working together with them.

The process of looking at the future made them grow naturally because they became able to find and improve their issues on their own. My team as a whole became very active and performed extremely well to be consistently recognized as one of the top teams in the company. Every time I was assigned to a different division, I applied the same method. Whether it was the sales or administrative department, my team's activities were revitalized. More specifically, I observed the following changes:

- The team's atmosphere became more cheerful and lively.
- Teamwork improved.
- The job got done more quickly (more productive, less overtime).
- Their activities resulted in greater sales.

Things that I have been practicing are the basis of *Feedforward*, which will be explained in this book. While cognitive science is the backbone of this method, you do not need to learn a difficult theory to practice it. For those who are interested in the theory and want to further improve their feedforward skills, more detailed explanations will be given in the latter half of this book. Please remember that feedforward begins with thinking and talking about your future.

This book presents how to use the *Feedforward Method* in an easy-to-understand manner. The book is organized in two parts: Part I, Feedforward Basics – Quick Start and Part II, The Path to Become an Advanced Feedforwarder. It is designed for you to be able to start practicing Feedforward immediately after reading Part I.

The secret of *Feedforward* is to *think from the future*. It is very different from the conventional way of discussion in which you start thinking about the past and present status. In contrast, feedback that many companies use is a typical method of starting to think about the past and present status first.

When I was young and right after I joined a foreign-capital company in Japan, my new boss, who was a westerner, asked me in English, "Mr. Hisano, please give me your feedback if you notice anything. It will help me and the organization get better." It was my first time learning the word feedback and I understood its meaning. As he was a board member of the company, he impressed me as a very broad-minded person. Being young at that time, I took his words seriously and I gave him a lot of feedback. He always welcomed my feedback and thanked me for it. We developed a good relationship.

On the other hand, I had a difficult experience with a different manager. He was also a westerner. He asked me, "Mr. Hisano, if you have any good ideas, please feel free to tell me. Feedback is also welcome, and please let me know what you think." However, in actuality, he did not want to hear my feedback. Without realizing his true feelings at that time, I actively provided a lot of ideas as he requested, and I gave him my feedback on what I thought would be helpful. I didn't get a good response from him. After a while, I was transferred to a different division. As I was performing well and producing good results, I felt it strange that I was removed from that team.

In retrospect, I realized that he was probably feeling annoyed with receiving my ideas and opinions so often. I had tried hard to give him my feedback because he asked for it. Perhaps, I should not have accepted his words so faithfully. As I was demoted afterward, I thought that he must have really disliked my feedback.

Feedback can work positively. However, from my experiences, I feel feedback could negatively affect our interpersonal relationships if we are not careful about its use. In many cases, feedback includes information that the receiver does not necessarily want to hear. Therefore, for most people it is difficult to accept feedback.

These days, people often emphasize the need for and importance of feedback as well as one-on-one or one-to-one meetings. Such meetings are certainly valuable. However, practicing one-on-one meetings is not as easy as you think. You need to properly prepare for the meeting. Especially, Japanese people in general are not so good at straightforward communications. Naturally, they are not so comfortable with feedback either.

As seen in the example of my previous boss, not only the Japanese but also western people seem to be disliking feedback. I also asked a few foreigners about feedback, and they did not like it either. An appropriate approach for receiving feedback seems to be listening to whatever information is given to you and pretending to be calm, even if the information includes something that you don't really wish to hear.

Feedback as a giver may also cause a problem as you may not know the receiver's true feelings because he/she may appear to be accepting your feedback. This is a story I once heard from a manager of the personnel department. He said, "There was an employee who I thought had great potential for advancement, but he has not been promoted as of yet. I was wondering why. The reason seemed to be related to an episode in which the person gave his feedback to the president (then a division manager). The president did not like the feedback, and he still has bad feelings toward the employee."

Feedback is a very difficult technique, as it can lead to the receivers recurrently looking at the past and recalling the ill feelings once again. This process can be upsetting to the receivers. When you look at the past, your brain replays your memory associated with your experience and further strengthens the reality of that event. As a result, the momentum to move toward the future is lost. This is a known fact based on cognitive science.

Of course, the goal of feedback is to create a better future by reviewing the past to identify the positive aspects to be continued and the necessary areas to be improved. However, it is difficult to use feedback effectively, as it tends to bind us to the past.

So, what I would like to suggest is *Feedforward*. I define *Feedforward* as follows:

Feedforward is a technique to encourage people, who tend to be stuck in the past and the current situation, to shift their focus to their future and take action to move forward. Feedforward begins with communication and observation to understand and accept the receivers' situation and their feelings that are associated with what is happening to them.

Feedforward helps individuals and organizations achieve high performance. I sincerely hope that this book will help you create a wonderful future for yourself.

*November 2023, Kazuyoshi Hisano*

# PART I

# Feedforward Basics Quick Start

Part I presents the basic concepts and practical methods of Feedforward. Once you complete Part I (Chapters 1-3), you will be able to immediately start using Feedforward in your life. The cognitive science aspects and more advanced techniques of Feedforward are described in Part II Chapters 4-6).

CHAPTER 1

# Miracles Created by Feedforward

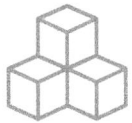

## 1.

### Top-level athletes are Feedforward thinkers

**Victory in Women's Soccer World Cup by Nadeshiko Japan and Feedforward thinking**

*Feedforward Thinking* refers to the following two activities:
Looking to the future rather than the past or present.
Working toward that future.

By doing so, creating more value, results, and happiness. Since feedforward thinking is simply looking to the future and working on it, anyone can easily acquire this skill. As you learn and use it, you can improve your life and the lives of those around you.

Some people naturally seem to be Feedforward thinkers. For example, top-level athletes have good habits of looking to the future and working toward it. Winning an upset victory with feedforward thinking in a desperate, critical situation is not so unusual.

In 2011, the team named *Nadeshiko Japan* became the first Japanese team to win the FIFA (translate from French as International Federation of Association Football) women's championship game, which was played in Germany. It was indeed a very close, last-minute victory.

The championship game was US against Japan. The US team was taking control of the game. This was bad news as the record of the Japanese women's team against the US was 0 wins, 21 losses, and 3 ties. They had never won before. Most people might have thought, based on past results, that it would be impossible for the Japanese team to win.

Indeed, it was a tough game. The Japanese team was fiercely attacked by the US team from the beginning and received numerous hits by Lauren Cheney and Abby Wambach. Japan persistently defended against them, but Alex Morgan made a successful shot on the right corner of the goal - giving the US a one goal lead at 69 minutes into the match. Wambach was confident about her US team's victory with this first point.

On the other hand, Homare Sawa, the captain of the Japanese team, encouraged her team by saying, "Don't give up! Let's go!" It was the message to look to the future. Her voice fired up the players to keep their hopes up, "We can still win," she kept on saying. The Japanese team patiently played the game, and in the 81st minute, Aya Miyama responded quickly to the ball cleared by the US just in front of the goal; shooting with her left foot she scored for the tie.

The game continued with the score tied and went into extra time. The US team players, Wambach and Morgan, were getting close to the Japanese goal. The result was predictable. They ended the first half of extra time, with the seamless connection by Wambach to Morgan's excellent pass to send the U.S. to a 2–1 lead again. When you allow the opponent to lead the score in extra time, it is exceedingly difficult to recover. This can easily break a team's spirit. Wambach thought they had surely won the game.

However, Nahomi Kawasumi and Yuki Nagasato shared the same sentiment with one another, "It's much more fun in a challenging situation like this!" And Miyama told herself "The most important time is what's next." The team players were always looking to the future. This made their comeback possible. In the latter half of extended time, the Japanese team tied the game when Miyama sent to Sawa a corner kick near the post.

The game inevitably progressed into penalty kicks. Japan's coach Norio Sasaki smiled and told them "Go and have fun!" Japan led 3 to 1, giving them their first win at the Women's World Cup Championship. We know that feedforward thinking had taken root among the team members, providing the power to bring them a successful outcome.

### Enjoy every moment at Koshien Stadium!

This is a story of Daisuke Matsuzaka, a former professional baseball pitcher in Japan and the US, when he was playing baseball at his high school. Matsuzaka was the ace pitcher at Yokohama High School. He was named the *Monster of the Heisei Era* after he pitched a complete game in the 80th Japan's National High School Baseball Championship (1998). In a single game during the quarterfinals, Matsuzaka threw 250 pitches in 17 innings in a win over PL Gakuen. The 250 pitches are equivalent to two games of pitching. In the interview after the game, Matsuzaka told the media that "I won't pitch tomorrow."

As predicted, the next day in the semifinals against Meitoku Gijuku High School, Matsuzaka started the game in the left field. Two sophomores at Yokohama High School were pitching in this game. The Meitoku batters were very aggressive and led the game with the score of 6-1 over Yokohama in the top of the 8th inning. At this point, many people believed in Meitoku would be victorious. In this critical situation, coach Motonori Watanabe told the team, "It's difficult to turn this game over in the two remaining innings, so just enjoy every moment of your experience at

Koshien!" He made the players relax by saying that it was difficult to turn this game over with only two innings left and then encouraged them to enjoy their *future* in this game.

And guess what? In the bottom of the 8th inning, Yokohama returned strong and scored 4 quick runs. In the top of the 9th inning, Yokohama sent Matsuzaka to the mound as a relief pitcher. He threw a no-hitter (one strikeout, one walk, and double play), holding the opponents scoreless. In the bottom of the 9th inning Yokohama made several hits, and in the end, they walked away with a miraculous victory.

When you are in the clutch, if you focus on analyzing the situation by thinking over the causes which led you to such a situation, you won't receive the power to fight. You will probably lose the fight before you have even started. The reason why they are the top athletes is that they look to the future – they have the ability to turn around a critical situation in their favor.

# 2.

## Envision your future even in the most desperate of circumstances

---

**If you can't believe in your future, you will break down physically and mentally**

*Man's Search for Meaning* by Viktor E. Frankl is a book for finding purpose and strength in times of great despair.

The author, a psychiatrist and psychologist, authored the book based on his experience in a Nazi concentration camp. In this book there is a line, "Forces beyond your control can take away everything you possess except one thing, your freedom to choose how you will respond to the situation." This means that we can decide how we respond to each situation, even if we find ourselves in extremely challenging circumstances. We have the freedom to envision our own future.

Viktor Frankl defines the condition of prisoners as having a *provisional existence of unknown limit.* In a bad situation where we don't know when this bad situation will end, and we think about the possibility that it may never end, it is difficult for us to live with purpose. We don't think we can live our life looking to the future. The book depicts that in the concentration camp, most prisoners closed their hearts and dwelled on the past. With their loss of belief in their future, they were doomed to undergo mental and physical decay. They remained lying down in their own excrement and eventually stopped moving altogether.

In such an extreme condition, Viktor Frankl succeeded in rising above the situation. All that oppression became the object of an interesting psychoscientific study undertaken by himself. More specifically, he envisioned the future where he, himself, was lecturing to his students after his release from the death camp. He went into further detail and envisioned giving his students lectures on the psychological lessons he had learned during his torture. He kept his hope for the future alive, even when his status was defined as having only a provisional existence.

Let's talk about the Toul Sleng Genocide Museum located in Phnom Penh, the capital of Cambodia. This facility is the site of the S21 security prison during the People's Republic of Kampuchea, governed by the Khmer Rouge (Communist Party of Cambodia). This is the time when Pol Pot was the dictator. During this era about 20,000 people were imprisoned and only eight people survived. I had a chance to interview Chum Mey, one of the survivors. He shared these words with me, "I only thought about tomorrow. I only thought about survival."

Of course, I don't mean to say that you can survive if you merely think about the future. However, if you are trapped with the past and present, your mind and body are driven into a corner. If you think about the future, it increases your chances for survival – I believe this to be true.

# 3.

## People who lost their confidence were reborn by Feedforward

### My family became healthy again by looking to the future

As I mentioned in the Prologue, I have learned the benefits of feedforward thinking from my own experience. When one of my family members became ill, out of a need to help, I read every medical book I could get my hands on. Also, I learned about the brain by becoming an apprentice to Dr. Tomabechi. Fortunately, the illness of my family member was cured completely. My family member began to feel better again by learning the power of imagining the future.

## What is *Feedforward*?

Let me explain once again how I define *Feedforward*.

1. First, understand the situation through communication and observation of those who tend to get stuck in the past and present.
2. Next, empathize with what is happening to the other person and what they are feeling.
3. Then, support the person in a way where they move their consciousness to the future and help them work toward it.

The method of the series of steps one, two, and three, is called *Feedforward*. Though *Feedforward* is a technique backed up by cognitive science, it is not difficult. Anyone can start practicing it. All you need is to look to the future and work toward it. I feel strongly about wanting to promote and establish *Feedforward Thinking* in the world. I am confident that it can contribute in a way where many people can achieve the ultimate results they strive for and feel wholehearted happiness.

## A businessman who once fell from the corporate ladder ended up winning the new-business competition

Let me introduce the case of Mr. A (male, 52 years old), who works for a famous Japanese manufacturer. He was an overseas office president for some years. Due to the economic downturn in the country, he was forced to execute a series of layoffs within his office. He completed his assignment in downsizing the overseas office. He later returned to headquarters. Downsizing his organization was not what he wanted, but he completed it because it was an order from above. What he experienced after returning to Japan was unexpected as he found himself in a position that was undesirable.

Since he believed that he was a successful upper-management-team player, he thought he would be a top candidate for further advancement within the company. He expected to move to a reasonable position after finishing the assignment overseas, even though the office he managed ended up shrinking. Nevertheless, what the personnel department offered him was not something he had anticipated. He felt devastated that they removed him from their executive management track. Mr. A felt that his professional career was over. Not only did he lose his motivation to work, but his health also deteriorated. That's when Mr. A came to see me for help.

I remember clearly that he looked very depressed. He said, "I have been working very hard since I joined this company immediately after my college graduation. My income increased to a certain point, but now I don't see a future."

I answered, "I understand…What do you really want to do now?"

Mr. A looked a little bit surprised. He reacted, "What do I really want…? I've never thought about it before. I genuinely believed that all I should do is to work hard and have faith in the company. However, now I see a reality that is totally different from what I had believed in, so I am at a loss about what I should do."

"I see," I said, "But the fact that you are talking to me now probably means that you are wanting to do something about it."

"Yes, I think so." He was just about to stand in front of a door to the future that he had never imagined before.

I said to him, "Let's take some time to figure this out. You will know what you want eventually."

When I saw him the next month, surprisingly he looked really happy.

Mr. A said, "After the last session with you, I applied my thoughts to what we discussed, and I feel now that I have started seeing the future."

"That's great. What happened?"

"Well, my goal was to become the first board member among my colleagues. That is why it was very hard to accept my most recent personnel assignment, which is really a demotion. For the past few months, I kept looking back to find the reasons why I was removed from the core management group. I wondered what possible reason there could be for me to be removed as a key player, especially after following the headquarters' order to lay-off my team. I thought it might be because I waited for a while before executing the layoff. This, of course, was because I was worried about my employees' future. Or it might have been my attitude toward challenging others; I didn't like to go with the flow. In any case I thought my colleagues seemed to be better at handling it."

I said, "I hear you. So, what do you really want to do?"

"Well, I want to live for myself, not for the company. Since I joined this company right after graduating from college, I devoted myself to the company and never questioned it."

## He felt happy again and started seeing the future

Mr. A smiled and said, "I have a business I want to start when I retire. That has been only a dream for retirement. But I realize that what I really want to do exists around that idea."

"I see. You found what you really want."

"Of course, I thought about staying with this company because I had already worked there so many years. Also, I have job inquiries from several other companies. But what I want to focus on now is thinking about the possibilities of a new business venture I want to get into."

"Wow, that is major progress. Wonderful!"

Since then, Mr. A has become full of energy to the point of saying, "Instead of quitting my company, I'll enter the company's business competition with my new business idea." He told me that he had this idea almost 20 years ago but had forgotten all about it.

This idea came back to him because he kept asking himself, "What do I want to do next?" For example, a business model for his new business idea existed in Europe. So, Mr. A traveled to Europe during his summer vacation to do research on the new business idea. He made an appointment with the European company, met with the manager in person, and gathered information for his business model.

After he returned to Japan, he continued to meet the stakeholders of his new business idea. After work and during weekends, he met with these people who were involved in new business development and better prepared himself for his future business proposal. While he continued these activities for some time, he started noticing that his feelings shifted toward enjoying his work at the company. When he saw things from a much higher perspective, he realized that his current job would also help him to develop his new business.

One year later, after his decision, he finally entered the company's business competition where he took first place! As the winner, he was given approval to start up his proposed business and received funds from the company to do it. Past winners of this contest were the younger generation, mostly in their 20s and 30s, so people cheerfully applauded him, calling him *a star of the middle-aged generation.*

Here we see a person, who once fell out of the mainstream management track in the company, due to heavy involvement in the restructuring of the company, to later revive his career by looking to the future.

### Confidence was regained by a woman whose habitual phrase was "I want to die," and "I want to dissolve like a bubble"

Ms. B (female, 41 years old) is working as a representative in the public relations department at a foreign capital company in Japan. When she came to me for a consultation, she appeared to be an energetic career-minded person. However, in reality, she told me that she couldn't find any meaning for her existence. She was single and popular among men. She was not interested in marriage, mostly because of the family environment in which she grew up in. She did not have confidence in any aspect of her life and was filled with worries and anxieties. Her habitual phrases were "I want to die," and "I want to dissolve like a bubble."

I asked her: "What do you really want to do?"

She replied, "There is nothing I want to do."

She paused a moment and looked as though she was remembering something.

She said, "I want to learn piano."

I said, "You do. That's nice."

Our first meeting concluded there.

The next time I saw her, the conversation went as follows:

"Well, piano was not a good idea. I don't have time to play."

"I see. Then, what do you really want to do?"

"What I want to do is... to help others solve their problems."

"I see. Well then, how about trying that idea?"

When I saw her the next time, she told me:

"Solving someone else's problem is not what I want to do. There's no way I can do that."

"I see. Well then, what do you genuinely want to do?"

For some time, our conversations went on as the ones above. On the surface, it looked as though we were not making progress, since we carried out our conversations back and forth in this manner. I did, however, notice something interesting. By encouraging her consciousness to look to the future, her face started looking much brighter, and she stopped saying "I want to die," or "I want to dissolve like a bubble."

A few months later, Ms. B finally found exactly what she wanted to do.

She said, "I feel that I am starting to see what I am looking for. I love animals. I want to build a facility for homeless animals."

"That is wonderful. What kind of facility would you like to build?"

Selecting her words carefully, Ms. B explained the following to me. "First, while I continue my current job, I will start building my personal network and knowledge, collecting funds and so forth. What I am trying to create is a very big project, so I must prepare for it well. And I want to brush up on my English because I think it would help me greatly in many different situations. After all, I am working in a foreign-capital company, and I should take advantage of this English-speaking environment.

She changed into a positive and cheerful person. It surprised the people around her. A year ago, the person who used to say, "I want to die," and "I want to dissolve like a bubble," now says, "I am great. Life is fun!" She is energetic, confident, and lively.

She told me recently that people often say to her, "You are such a positive person." Such comments initially surprised her as she had never been described in this way before. With a smile, she now says, "I am getting used to it."

The secret is very simple. *Think and talk about the future.* With my intention to help her look into her future, all I did was to keep asking her, "What do you really want to do?" Feedforward is very simple, and it has a great effect.

So, let's put your consciousness toward your future. What do you really want to do?

CHAPTER 2

# Japanese Who Get Stuck in the Past

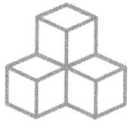

## 1.

### Why Feedback does not work?

**Improve your work by telling the unpleasant truth**

There are so many books that talk about how we should communicate with people. Everyone is looking for the most appropriate way to communicate with people, including those of different generations. One of the popular methods, these days, is the use of *feedback*.

Feedback originally came from the term used in Feedback Control Theory, which is a part of the theory behind Control Engineering. The term is described as something (such as information or electricity) that is returned back to a machine, a system, or a process. This is why we speak in terms of a feedback loop. The business world then extrapolated this concept to communication, and the term feedback has become popular and commonly used ever since.

For example, a supervisor evaluates team members, and the results are to reflect in each member's salary increase or promotion, or more directly, providing specific praise – this is called *feedback*. There are a lot of definitions of feedback. Here is another definition, *to improve the work or performance of an individual by telling them the unpleasant truth when they are underperforming.*[1]

Generally, feedback means sharing your thoughts candidly to others in certain situations. One process is to start with sharing the good points and areas needing improvement to a person who just gave a presentation. In such a case, simply telling the facts without emotional attachment is considered important.

## Feedback can be stressful for both, those who give and those who receive

Generally speaking, feedback does not work so well in most offices. The purpose of feedback is to move work forward and improve, but unfortunately, the intended effect is not

---

1 Defined by Atsushi Nakahara, Associate Professor at Tokyo University.

often realized. I think the biggest factor to explain this difficulty is that *giving and receiving feedback* is not easy. Both those who give and those who receive feedback must have considerable competence and capacity.

Let me share my experience here as an example of some feedback that worked. When I worked for a foreign-affiliated company in Japan, my supervisor sometimes asked me for feedback on ideas and presentations. We exchanged our opinions daily, but when he asked me to give him feedback, he was more serious. If I casually expressed what I felt, he would say, "I am asking you for specific issues and areas for improvement, not just your impressions."

So, I would get serious and tell him my straightforward opinions that could often be unwelcome by his ears, though he had asked for it. My supervisor appeared to be somewhat irritated when I expressed my honest opinions, but he was in general, appreciative. However, such a case is rare.

If you set goals that are clear and high-enough and work straight toward them, you would be more accepting of feedback given by others in the areas in which you need improvement. However, such people are very rare. For this reason, many people say that when their boss gives them feedback, they feel resistant and depressed.

On the other hand, the people who are giving feedback also feel stressed. The same is true when a supervisor gives feedback to his/her team members. Undoubtedly, there is the possibility that they will hate the supervisor for their harsh feedback.

After all, **feedback has a strong psychological toll on both the giver and the receiver.** Also, when you receive feedback, you must think about multiple things. Feedback is based on the premise that specific areas can be improved. These areas are pointed out, such as procedures and skills needed for the work, by the giver. When you receive it, you need to think of it as a statement for your improvement. Try not to react emotionally to whatever is said. After this you can then choose your reaction to the feedback.

Whatever the feedback statements may be, you must bear them in mind, saying to yourself, "Don't get angry," "Don't get depressed," or "Don't ignore this information." Furthermore, it is your responsibility to judge how appropriate the points raised are. You need to think carefully about how much you want to incorporate the feedback you received.

Related to this, some people seem to think, "When I was young, I was raised with harsh feedback, so it's natural for me to give strict feedback to others." This is a type of thinking stuck in the past. I understand a little about their sentiment, but we should think about the past as the past and think about how we will be able to interact with those people around us to succeed as an organization or as an individual.

# 2.

## A culture that welcomes feedback, versus a culture that doesn't

---

### Feedback does not fit so well with the Japanese people

I don't think the method of feedback fits so well with the Japanese people. This is because Japan does not have a culture of speaking frankly like in the West. To speak frankly means you put aside hesitations toward others and express frank opinions. However, I don't think it's possible for Japanese people, who value harmony, to speak frankly without hesitation in a relationship that isn't close enough yet.

From the age of 1 to 6, I spent time in the United States because of my father's work. Later, I transferred to a Japanese elementary school in the second semester of my first year of elementary school. Shortly thereafter there was something that bothered me during class, so I inadvertently said, "Teacher, I don't think so." The classroom fell silent.

The teacher looked at me with anger, and my classmates were nervous. "Why?" I thought. I was imagining that if I said, "I don't think so," the teacher would ask me "What do you think?" then I would answer "I don't think so because of such and such reasons."

However, he scolded me saying, "What are you saying?" I couldn't help but say, "Why? I just said what I thought."

This made the teacher even angrier. "If you keep saying such things, go out to the hallway." He scolded me even harder.

Still unsure, I went out into the hallway and thought, "What did I do wrong?" Even though I was a child, I wondered if the way I made my comments was the reason I got scolded. So, when the same thing happens again, I should change how I say it and add the reason why I think differently something like, "Teacher, I don't think so because such and such reasons."

Oh well, I tried this and I got scolded again. This was my first lesson, it was that I would get scolded when I disagreed (i.e., was giving honest feedback). Also, I learned that people who receive disagreement (the receivers of feedback) often feel quite bad.

## Western people exchange opinions regularly

When I was very young and lived in America, "I don't think so" was a part of normal conversation. When I asked people about something, "What do you think?" I got responses like "That's not right." "I don't think so." or "Isn't it better this way?" Even in Japan, pre-school children up to 5 years old clearly say, "I don't like that," and "That's not right." They pretty much say what they think until around that age, then they stop being so frank.

When you say, "I don't think so" in Japan, people tend to take it as implying, "That's wrong." It took me quite a while before I got this feeling. Since I returned to Japan at the age of 6, I struggled figuring out how I should communicate with others. During my junior high school days, I finally started understanding the nuances. It indeed took me a long time. Moreover, it was only recently that I felt that I had mastered just the right communication responses.

I feel that many people in Japan tend to equate *one's own opinion* with *one's own character*. Those who think that way often get angry when their opinion is disagreed with, because they feel as if their personality is being denied and are left with a feeling of rejection.

Also, Japanese people tend not to say things very clearly. Even so, they can communicate with one another because they have a mutual understanding that communication includes the meaning hidden between the lines.

## We need skills to convey our thoughts

Since I returned to Japan in the first grade of elementary school, I struggled to communicate with others until I moved again, this time to England at the age of 14. Up until then, my experiences had been that when I expressed my honest opinions in response to the questions I was being asked, the other person frequently became annoyed. I had been wondering what was wrong in sharing my true thoughts. When I was in the upper grades of elementary school, I was bullied and sometimes ostracized by my peers.

Luckily, when I was in the third year of junior high school, I was able to say what I wanted to say again. That is only because I was able to go to a Japanese school instead of a local school in England. It was somewhat in the Japanese culture, but most of my classmates had lived abroad for a long time, so I was able to get along with everyone more comfortably than when I was in Japan. Perhaps it was the teachers dispatched from Japan had the hardest time in dealing with us. I think there were many times when they seemed to be upset with us as unruly children.

Then one day, I came across a book on my father's bookshelf called *How to Win Friends and Influence People* by Dale Carnegie. This book changed my life greatly.

The high school I entered was a Japanese boarding school called Rikkyo School in England. It is a long-established school, where it attracts the children from the overseas employees of Japanese trading companies, banks, manufacturers, embassies, etc. The school was attended by not only the students from the UK but also globally from other European countries, as well as the Arab and African countries.

We high school students were still very young and lived in the dorm away from our parents. For us youngsters, our relationship with our friends was often a cause of distress. I spent my time thinking about how we can communicate smoothly with each other. If we call it the worries of youth, that's certainly so, but this was a serious matter for us.

*How to Win Friends and Influence People* is a very famous book, so many of you may have read it. This book teaches us that we need skills to communicate something to others. In the book I found 37 principles to influence people, including three fundamental techniques in handling people and six ways to make people like you. I wrote down these 37 principles on a piece of paper and carried them around so I could look at them frequently. I was perhaps a bit unusual as a high school student.

The book began with an episode of the criminal's letter saying, "Under my coat is a weary heart, but a kind one – one that would do nobody any harm." It talked about how "Few of the criminals in jail regard themselves as bad men. They are just as human as you and I. So, they rationalize, and they explain."

In that chapter, the author wrote, "Instead of condemning people, let's try to understand them. Let's try to figure out why they do what they do. That's a lot more profitable and intriguing than criticism." He summarized the chapter with some key advice, "Don't criticize, condemn or complain."

I learned important lessons of communication: respecting others, listening well, and recognizing that the other person always has his/her reasons for what they say and do.

As for feedback, if you understand fully what the other has to say and respect it, I believe you can give and receive feedback well. But again, feedback requires higher skills to perform it effectively. Further to this the person who receives it must be ready for it.

I was raised in an environment where giving feedback was common, but that method may not be suitable for other countries or cultures. In particular, I feel feedback is not so conducive to the Japanese culture. Since I was experiencing difficulty with providing feedback, I came to think that we need to develop other methods.

# 3.

## Feedback consumes your energy for reflection

---

### Think from the past, or think from the future

Feedback is designed to improve future activities, but its focus tends to be on the evaluation of past events, and I don't think that people are using this method effectively. Therefore, some people are afraid of getting feedback or hesitant to give feedback. The biggest reason for this is that the feedback is based on looking into the past.

On the contrary, Feedforward looks at the future. While feedback is based on the premise that *time flows from the past toward the present*, Feedforward is based on a different premise and direction, *time flows from the future toward the present*. Feedback is based on comments provided about past events (even if it's just the immediate past). Therefore, it has the opposite nature from Feedforward, which is communication about the future.

Of course, the purpose of feedback is to improve future activities, so it includes an aspect of Feedforward in the long run. However, its first step is toward the past, the weight is on looking back. Feedback is forecasting-like thinking. Predicting the future like *the world will become like this* from the current or past data, which is called *forecasting*. When we use forecasting to think about our future, distinguishing the highly probable future from existing factors becomes important. Diverse ideas and imagination can also slacken.

On the other hand, *Feedforward is backcasting-like thinking.* You place your perspective in the future, from where you look back to the present – we call *backcasting*. When backcasting, you look to the future and imagine your own desirable future. Because you create your future from your will power, *wanting to become like this*, you can think of many possible future images. Thus, you can freely imagine your future, so you feel excited.

Feedforward promotes *future-oriented thinking*. You view your time starting from the future: You make decisions on the future, the time flows from the future to the present, and the decided future becomes materialized. This is the perspective we take.

## Feedback hinders you from moving forward

**The weakest point of feedback is that it starts from the past.** Feedback starts from talking about the past within the timeline from the past to the future. Once looking back, the past is finished, we look at the future. In this process, you consume most of your energy on past events (analysis and validation), and you run out of energy before you can even start thinking about the future. Also, after you list all

## Feedforward and Feedback

| | Feedforward<br>Future improvement | Feedback<br>Future improvement |
|---|---|---|
| | FUTURE | PAST |
| **Starting Point** | Creation of future memories | Reexperience of the past failures<br><br>Strengthened past memories |
| **State of the Brain** | Activation of the prefrontal cortex | Activation of the limbic system (suppressed activities of the prefrontal cortex) |
| **Brain Chemicals** | Dopamine release to the prefrontal cortex<br><br>Creative idea generation<br><br>Higher performance | Suppressed dopamine release<br><br>Increased noradrenalin release<br><br>Suppressed thinking<br><br>Lower performance |
| **Psychological State** | Fun, happy | Difficult, boring |

items that need to be get done through the process of ana-lyzing/evaluating the past and current situations, you feel more obligated to work on what is necessary and lack then the necessary power to move forward toward the next stage which relates to the future.

What is happening inside the brain when you investigate the past is that you reexperience your failures and restrengthen the memories of those failures of your past. This tends to result in suppressing the activity of the prefrontal cortex, which is the source of positive energy and creativity, and activates instead the limbic system, which controls our crisis response.

Here is an example. An organization utilized the feedback method when they tried to turn the company around. They listed all their weaknesses and the areas needing improve-ment so that they can address their problems one by one. However, while they were making a list of their company's weaknesses, the members lost their confidence. Although they declared "We will improve this and that," they couldn't achieve what they intended, because they exhausted their energy before even starting to implement their improvements. Clearly, their prefrontal cortex was not activated by this activity.

If you use the feedforward method in the same situation, you can expect the prefrontal cortex of your brain to become very active and to generate full energy. In this situation, your creativity is enhanced resulting in the generation of many new ideas. Thus, you can expect to achieve desirable results.

# 4.

## FFA instead of PDCA

---

### PDCA also binds us to the past

I hear many people in Japan say that they have been implementing the PDCA cycle to their business, but it is not working so well for them. Of course, in the areas such as production control and quality control, I believe that a precise PDCA cycle is highly effective for problem-solving.

However, those companies that have difficulty with the PDCA cycle seem to be using it as an organizational program that aims for continuous business process improvement and refers to the feedback loop of activities: Plan ➡ Do ➡ Check ➡ Act.

---

**PDCA Cycle**

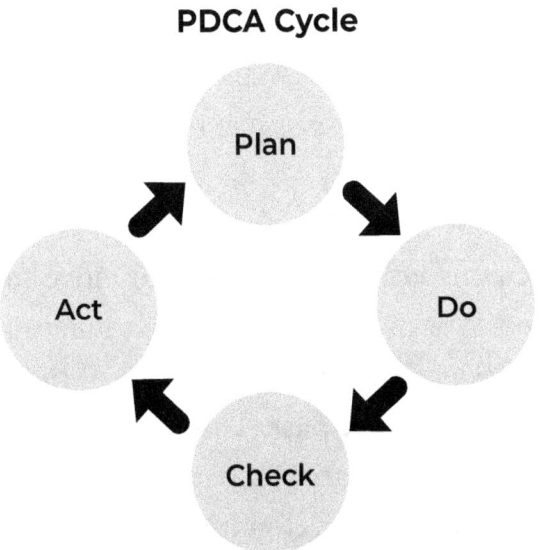

On the other hand, successful companies do not use the PDCA cycle as a stand-alone method. They adopt their PDCA practice to incorporate a feedforward mechanism into the cycle for materializing improvements for the future.

In this section, I will contrast PDCA, as commonly practiced, with Feedforward and introduce the approach of FFA (Feedforward Action).

For a long time, I have had a question about PDCA. I have been involved in business management in various capacities: I earned an MBA and have been working as a business consultant. Through these experiences, I am familiar with the concept and the aims of PDCA. Also, I know that applying PDCA is one of the requirements in ISO (International Organization for Standardization) certification. I had worked for the ISO certification body for a short while, so, I do understand the true meaning of PDCA for manufacturing and quality control, to which ISO is applied overall.

However, people have difficulty rotating the PDCA cycle well in the real world. PDCA does not work even if you try very hard. From my perspective, I see a clear reason for it, though other people may not be aware of it. The reason I observed as to why PDCA does not work well is that its concept contains both the intention to move forward and the intention to stay in the past at the same time.

**PDCA is designed based on reflection of the past, which is why it binds us in the past.** This is the same mechanism of feedback in that we are stuck in the past and unable to build our future. From a cognitive science point of view, intentionally reflecting on your past involves a risk that you won't have the energy remaining for building your future.

## Two out four steps in the PDCA process are reflection

The first step of the PDCA cycle "Plan" starts by making an improvement plan after analyzing the past and the company's current problems. It considers an estimated future state, but such an estimation is an extension of the current situation. We plan to create a better future, of course, but because PDCA starts with defining issues, it orients our thinking toward the issues of our past. This is a problem.

Another problem lies in the step *Check* after the *Do* step. Naturally, *Check* involves reflection. Here if you perform *Check*, which is the process of intentionally looking back at the past, it makes you stuck in the past even more strongly. Also, because of the *Check* step in the cycle, the *Plan* step is based on the *Check* step when you plan, which puts more weight on backward thinking and movement when you run the full PDCA cycle.

Simply put, **two of the four steps in the process are actions that put weight on reflection (the past)**. It is important to *take action* to achieve something. It is true that *Plan* and *Check* are necessary, but we shouldn't spend so much time on them.

Reflection meetings can make people's minds heavy. At school, there is a short meeting called "end of day homeroom" or "afternoon homeroom," or it may have been called "reflection time" in different parts of the world. This meeting is to reflect on what happened during the day, but normally it is a formality. The atmosphere tends to be dark, and the ideas and opinions that students have in that type of meeting are not applied later by the school system.

The same applies at work. The more seriously you reflect on what you did, the more difficult it becomes to move forward. As you dig into your weaknesses and bad points it will inevitably make your heart heavy. Also, the same as with feedback, most energy is consumed with past stories (analysis and evaluation), and you get tired before you can even get started in thinking about your future. As you analyze and evaluate the past and your current situation to make a list of action items that you must do, you become more obligated. This in turn keeps your brain away from functioning well in the area of moving forward.

I am going to explain this all in more detail in Part II, but this *sense of obligation* is troublesome. The sense of obligation which makes you feel like *you must do things* is called the *have-to* mindset. This is the opposite of *want-to*, which is the state you feel when *you are willing to do things*. To activate the prefrontal cortex, you need to work on things from the feeling of *want-to*, but PDCA often creates *have-to* feelings.

In fact, when each step of P, D, C, A has an assigned manager, the system appears to be functioning. However, because the problems such as *stuck in the past* and *feeling obligation* stay unsolved, your prefrontal cortex does not get activated. Therefore, it's difficult to achieve the desired results; besides, the organizational speed is slow.

## Feedforward Thinking is a
## Future-oriented Planning System

I would like to propose the *Feedforward* ➡ *Action* (FFA) process, to replace the PDCA concept.

FFA has significant advantages over PDCA in several respects. FFA may become a central concept in the future. Most successful people have always acted in an FFA-oriented fashion. They do not live by PDCA.

With FFA,

1. You set a goal.
2. It activates the brain and makes you realize the necessary methods to achieve your goals (inspiration).
3. When you try to take actions, *subconscious reflection* will occur, and you will notice the necessary improvement points/areas in the way that you have done things so far.

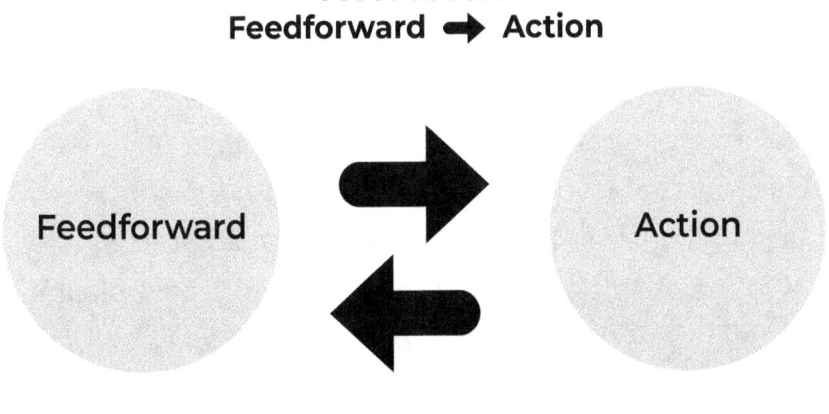

**FFA Process**
**Feedforward ➡ Action**

Feedforward    Action

Feedforward ➡ Action Process
**Framework for Shaping the Future**

4. Proceed with actions that incorporate the improvement points you have noticed.

5. While reviewing the goal from time to time, we incorporate newly noticed points for improvement into our actions, and further improve the quality of our actions.

These steps are repeated. They are the basics of FFA. In FFA, it is clearly stated to start with "goal setting," and from the cognitive science point of view, the effect of FFA is guaranteed.

## Subconscious Reflection is subsumed

Feedforward thinking is a future-oriented planning. Feedforward subsumes Goal Setting ➡ Subconscious Reflection. Future-oriented planning can be divided into long-term and short-term.

Long-term future-oriented planning, as I have already mentioned, will follow this cycle: *Goal Setting* ➡ *Subconscious Reflection* ➡ *Action*. While the framework of FFA is a simple format of *Feedforward* ➡ *Action*, *Feedforward* subsumes Goal-setting and Subconscious reflection. You repeat this cycle. While you take action, you will return to *Feedforward* as many times as you need to and take action again accordingly.

On the other hand, Short-term future-oriented planning will follow this cycle: *Target Setting* ➡ *Subconscious Adjustment* ➡ *Action*.

When you set big goals, it is important for you to set smaller goals (targets). You must also know what exactly you should do in the immediate future. The same applies to your daily work. If you know where to begin, it gets easier to move forward. For this purpose, we use the term *Target* as a short-term goal, meaning to aim at.

While having a long-term goal of *I want to be like this*, we set targets as short-term goals such as yearly, quarterly, monthly, and weekly. By setting a specific target under the goal, the brain's subconscious starts bringing up a flash of intuition for a specific action.

If you execute the action that inspired you, the appropriate result will follow. While you are taking action, the brain continues to make subconscious adjustments for the action. Together with feedforward thinking, which includes reviewing the targets, the quality of the action will be further enhanced. This is the short-term FFA process.

A corporate executive switched to FFA from PDCA that had been practiced in the workplace. The executive commented, "When we were using PDCA to analyze the current situation and formulate a plan, things hardly moved forward. After switching to FFA, employees began to think independently. They got involved in discussions more actively and started to take actions more quickly. Also, as we set a goal using FFA, I began noticing my subconscious let me catch the information necessary to achieve the goal. I now feel I can always see what to do next. Before, I was always thinking hard (and sometimes holding my head) about what I should do next. After switching to FFA, all we need to do is to set goals and taking action while waiting for the next inspiration to come. It is a truly revolutionary change!"

What do you think? This corporate executive and many others experienced a big difference. This change is related

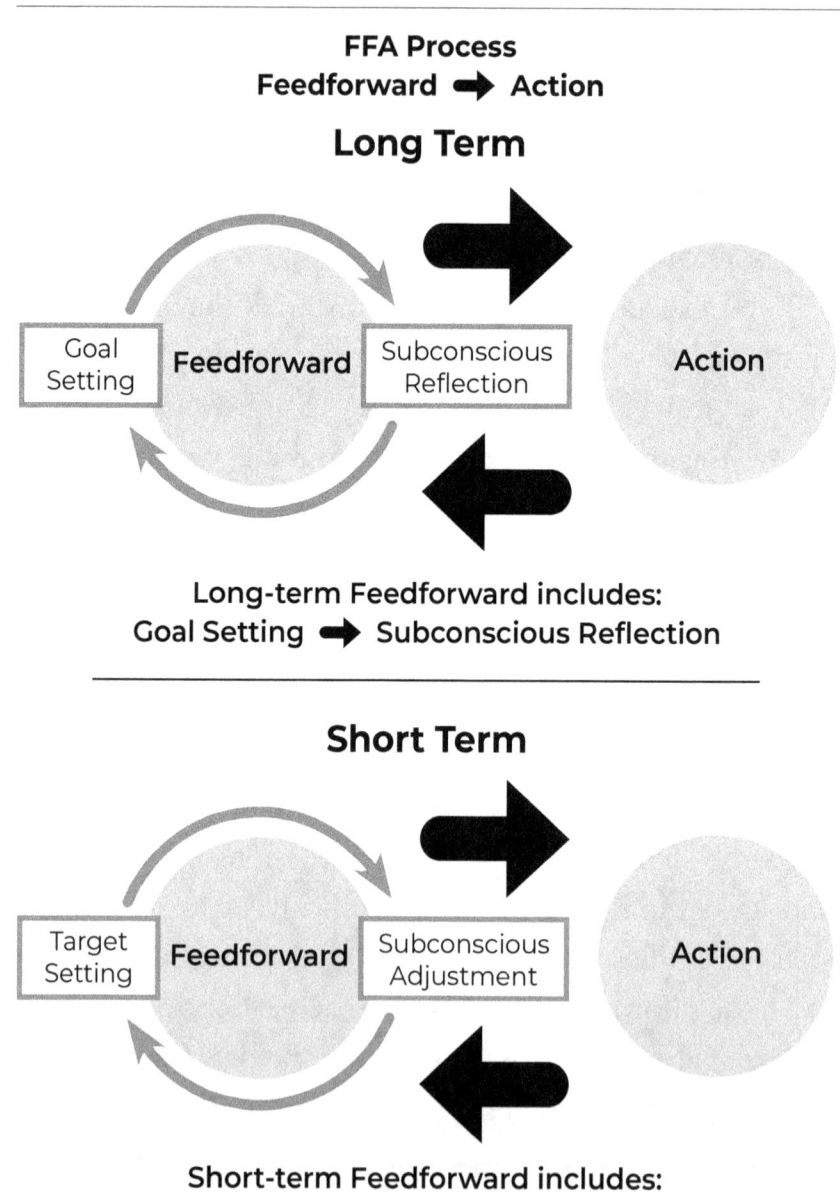

**FFA Process**
**Feedforward ➡ Action**

## Long Term

| Goal Setting | **Feedforward** | Subconscious Reflection | | **Action** |

**Long-term Feedforward includes:**
**Goal Setting ➡ Subconscious Reflection**

## Short Term

| Target Setting | **Feedforward** | Subconscious Adjustment | | **Action** |

**Short-term Feedforward includes:**
**Target Setting ➡ Subconscious Adjustment**

to how the brain works. Our brain only perceives what we think is important. In a part of the brain called the brainstem, there is the *RAS (Reticular Activating System)* that acts as a filter for information from the outside. This filtering function of RAS allows us to sense only what we recognize as important.

When you start thinking about the points needing reflection through feedback and PDCA, the brain regards this information needing reflection as important and collects it. As a result, you will end up with piles of information. During this process, what happens in your brain is that it begins to relive past unsuccessful experiences; repeatedly, and thus loses the energy to move forward and feels sluggish.

On the other hand, if you focus on the future and think about your goal in a feedforward way, the information in which you need to achieve your goals will keep coming to you. Inside your brain, the prefrontal cortex becomes more active, enhances your motivation, and brings out your extraordinary creativity.

How we use our brain makes a big difference between FFA and PDCA. FFA will change the way you approach your work. PDCA is an epoch-making invention in the 20th century and has contributed greatly to the development of the world, but it may be getting out of date.

## Goals don't have to be clear from the beginning

**The more you plan, the less it works.** I have seen this phenomenon at play in many cases.

When I was in elementary school, every year my school made us create a daily plan of how we saw ourselves spending summer break. I could follow my plan only for the first few days. After that I couldn't continue as planned, and the rest of the summer break became all free time. I wondered, "Maybe I'm no good at this because I can't continue following the plan." The few days I was able to stick to my plan were not so much fun, and I couldn't learn anything or come up with any ideas. From the moment I said to myself, "I give up on my plan," my summer break became fun.

There were times I studied for entrance exams. I would create a study plan, but I couldn't stick to it. I lost interest in my plan almost as quickly as I was making it. Eventually, I ended up studying the subjects that I felt I needed as they came to my mind, and I survived the several entrance exams that I took. For a long time, I wondered if planning was meaningful.

As a manager and the person in charge of corporate planning at multiple companies, I have personally been involved in creating various plans, such as five-year plans, three-year plans, annual budgets, and monthly budgets. I did it because it was a part of my job, but it wasn't fun for me.

*Without a plan, employees will not work.* At one point, I understood that the company was making plans because they believed in that method. It's a method or trick to make employees do things they don't necessarily want to do. This realization made me like the planning process even less at those companies.

Dr. Hideto Tomabechi and Mr. Lou Tice gave me valuable hints for my long-time skepticism about the effectiveness of the plan. These two people gave me the perspectives such as *Time comes from the future* (Dr. Tomabechi) and *Invent on the way* (Mr. Tice). A saying often said in a venture company is, "Think while running." It has been 15 years since I was introduced to these perspectives that made me feel "These perspectives must be it."

In a way, I, who disliked plans, had Dr. Tomabechi's and Mr. Tice's perspectives all along. I felt greatly supported and encouraged by their thoughts, and I have been living with the mindset of creating the future.

Feedforward and FFA (Feedforward ➡ Action) are the resulting methods that I compiled from my thinking, experimenting, experience, and producing results in the last 15 years. What I am saying may not be very new, but I believe it is new in the sense that these methods are formulated as a system.

I don't think that there are many people who achieved something because of their detailed planning. Rather, all the great people seemed to be successful because they had a big dream to begin with and continued taking actions toward it.

CHAPTER 3

# Feedforward Basics

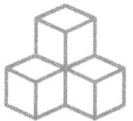

# 1.

## The reason Feedforward is necessary

### Importance of one-on-one meetings

The mainstream style of performance appraisal in Japan is to evaluate employees' performance, ability, contribution, etc. every six months or once every year. The results are reflected in salary increases and promotions. Targets are set at the beginning of the fiscal year, and evaluations are conducted at the end of the fiscal year through self-evaluation, evaluation by the manager, and further interviews with the manager.

This method was originally used in the United States, but since around 2012, many American companies such as Microsoft, GE (General Electric), Accenture, etc. have been abolishing such short-term and routinely scheduled personnel evaluations. The business environment is changing rapidly, and it is difficult to evaluate employees based on the goals set six months or one year ago. Well then, how should we conduct performance appraisals?

Recently, approaches that emphasize everyday communication have become more popular. One of them is a *one-on-one meeting* (sometimes called the one-to-one meeting, but I would like to call it *one-on-one* in this book.) It is intended to promote close communication with employees. In Silicon Valley, one-on-one meetings have taken root as a culture and are used as a human resource development method as well.

In one-on-one meetings, managers are supposed to carefully listen to their team members and give advice as needed. By providing a safe place to talk with each other openly and regularly, team members grow and communication within the company also becomes more active.

## Cheerful and fun interview tools

Many people recommend one-on-one meetings, but they don't necessarily explain the methodology clearly. When

HR asks managers to implement one-on-one meetings regularly, many of them don't know where to start. They are at a loss as to what to start talking about. Many of them are confused with how to integrate this with MBO (management by objective). In some cases, they end up just having small talk or letting their team members vent their complaints.

This situation hinders the original purpose of one-on-one, which is supposed to help managers understand the team members' status and promote their growth. In general, the one-on-one approach is intended to bring out the abilities of each individual using the three elements of teaching, coaching, and feedback.

During the meeting the agenda is to talk about the work that went well and work that didn't go well, and then the manager will ask questions like, "What did you learn from that?" or "How can you use your learning in the future?" The purpose of one-on-one is to think together. It's not a business report or progress management, so it's not a place to judge the success or failure of what they've done. And managers sometimes provide their feedback in the dialogue, saying something like "It looked like this to me, and this is what I thought about what you were doing."

If it is done well, one-on-one is very effective. Why not make it cheerful and fun, and not so formal as a job interview? You want to develop your company's talent and revitalize the company's internal communication. However, if there is a lot of feedback in the one-on-one meeting, that will inevitably create a heavy atmosphere because the focus will tend to go to the past and, in particular, what didn't go well. In that respect, I believe that the best way to conduct one-on-one meetings is the feedforward method presented in this book.

# 2.

## Introducing Feedforward into the company

---

### Feedforward looks to the future

By being conscious of and working toward the future, people will achieve results and become happy. As I mentioned earlier, I realized how wonderful future-oriented thinking was when my family member's illness was cured. So, I decided to introduce *Feedforward* to my team members at work.

All I did was hold monthly one-on-one meetings and kept asking, "What do you want to do next?" In the process of looking to the future, everyone was able to discover and improve their issues naturally, so they grew effortlessly. My team members became more active and involved, and my department's performance continued to improve. Every time I moved to a new department, I tried it there. And in each case my teams became more active, whether it was in the sales department or the administrative department.

This *Feedforward Method* is based on cognitive science, but it does not require you to learn difficult theories. An attractive point of *Feedforward* is that anyone can use it immediately. Despite its simplicity and ease of application, *Feedforward* is a profound system. The theory underlying it will be elaborated in the latter half of the book for those who are interested in using feedforward with greater understanding and more effective application. But first, I would like to show you that just *being conscious of the future* and *talking about the future* is enough to perform well at feedforward.

## How did I implement Feedforward?

When I introduced *Feedforward* to my department, I named our meeting, *Feedforward Meeting*. I proceeded as follows:

### 1. Briefing

First, I had everyone in my department gather for a briefing on *Feedforward*. I started by saying, "We will create a forum for everyone to contribute toward improving our department. This is called a feedforward meeting. This is not the time for me to give you feedback about your work. It is a time during which each of you can discuss what you want to do from now on. You can tell me anything you want to say. I will keep your secrets confidential. If you prepare what you want to talk about in advance, we can use our time effectively. You will meet me one-on-one, usually for 30 minutes. Please allow one hour for the first session, as I would like to have enough time to listen to you well." I shared this to all members of the department and got their consent to hold Feedforward meetings.

## 2. Scheduling

Next, I set a meeting date. Basically, I conducted a meeting for about 30 minutes per person every month. I made a timetable and secured time for each member to consult with them. As I mentioned earlier, I decided that the first session should be one hour for each employee. This is because I needed sufficient time to carefully listen to what my team members had accumulated to date.

When I first implemented the one-on-one meetings, my department had nearly 20 members. I tried to keep all meetings to 30 minutes per person as much as possible. However, I found that it was difficult to end the first and second sessions on time. We sometimes took almost an hour. My department had 20 people, so the longer meetings of approximately sixty minutes meant that nearly half of the week was accounted for. Despite this, I found that the effectiveness of these meetings was worth the effort. From the third meeting forward, I was able to finish each session in 30 minutes.

## The basic flow of Feedforward

As a premise of *Feedforward*, I believe that all employees, to a greater or lesser extent, want to contribute to the company as long as they belong to the company. If they hate the company, then they will quit. Even for some people who are a little undermotivated at the moment have feelings for the company and the organization, but you listen to them carefully to uncover this. If you bring such feelings out of them, they will naturally become a motivated person.

You will begin feedforward with words of appreciation such as: "Thank you for your hard work as always." "I know that you are having a hard time with recent projects but thank you for always delivering steady results." "Thanks to your attentiveness, our team's communication has improved, and I am always grateful."

Then, you explain, "The reason why I asked for your time today is to have a feedforward meeting, as I mentioned in our briefing session. We will do this once a month. Thank you for your understanding and support." After you explain things in this way, ask one or two questions as an icebreaker.

"What do you do on your days-off?"
"What is your interest on these days?"

These are good questions. And if you are a new manager who was recently transferred to the division, questions like "How many years have you been working for this company?" or "How many years ago were you assigned to this department?" are good, too. Have your team members talk enough and listen to them attentively.

## Asking questions that look to the future

Then ask them "What kind of work would you like to do in the future?" Some of you are lucky enough to have had your manager ask you this kind of question before. If so, you would be blessed with your company and your manager. For many people, this is a question that has never been asked before, so their reaction might be, "What?"

If your team members are in their first or second session, and sometimes even later in the sessions, they generally react to these questions by thinking, "It's taboo to say such things," and "I shouldn't be perceived as being dissatisfied with the work I am currently doing." That's why I believe people tend to make safe statements. It may be different if they are talking to their peers, with whom they feel they can be more candid. However, as they are usually wary of their manager, they tend to say many statements that are safe and maintain the status quo, such as "I want to do my best at my current job." This is when *Feedforward* becomes handy.

For example, you can explain, "There will be opportunities for personnel transfers within the company. I don't think you are likely to want to stay in this department indefinitely. If you were able to move to some other department in three years, what kind of work would you like to do? If I knew, I might be able to support you."

Or even in an organization with few personnel changes, you might say, "Of course, I am grateful that you are working hard in your current job, and I would like to ask you to continue to do so in the future. However, if you have any other interests to expand your skills, please let me know. There may be things that can be done within this department, and there may be things that can only be done in other departments. If you let me know your interests in advance, when the opportunity arises, we can further discuss what you want to do, and thereby I can recommend you for the job." By saying this you can make them look to the future, outside of the current situation, while also making them aware of possible benefits to themselves.

In the beginning, they are stiff, but as the sessions progress, they realize that a feedforward meeting is a safe space. They become comfortable talking more openly about a variety of things. At that time, the dialogue develops as follows:

### Example 1

Manager: What kind of job do you want to do in the future?

Team Member: I want to try ABC.

Manager: I see. How do you think you can achieve that?

### Example 2

Manager: What kind of job do you want to do in the future?

Team Member: I want to improve my skills of XYZ which I am currently working on.

Manager: I see. How do you think you can improve those skills?

Team Member: I think I need more experience performing more difficult tasks.

Manager: I understand. Are you ready to take that opportunity? Or, is there anything that I can do to help you with it?

In some cases, the employee might make a specific request such as "I want you to do such and such." But there may also be people who say, "I am fine for now. I will let you know when I need your help."

Furthermore, some people may talk about things that are not directly related to the business of the company. For example, "I want to win a triathlon," or "I want to work in the field of education," even though they are the printing industry. At such times, we must be careful to not say something like, "I'm talking about work," or "You can't do that work at our company." Instead, you can respond, "Good. How do you think you can do that?" Then, they start discussing what they have been thinking about and the ideas that they come up with at the moment. Of course, we must listen to those things as well.

The important thing here is to accept whatever the other person says. Even if it conflicts with your interests as a manager, you need to accept and listen attentively. Another circumstance is if your department is understaffed. In that case, it would be very difficult for you to see even one person leave due to relocation or opportunities that arise from a retirement. Even in such a case, you as a manager need to listen to and accept members who say, "I want to try a different job." The future belongs to every individual, so we have no choice but to respect what they want.

You as the manager will think about how you can help team members. You don't have to actively encourage them to change jobs, but if there is something the organization can do for them, especially in moving them in the direction they want (usually there is something), do your best. Sometimes you can support and negotiate their transfer to another division, and in some cases, they change jobs on their own, but that's just the way it is. The missing position can usually be taken care of by making a request for HR to fill the position.

Some people worry that if they listen too much to their team members, more people will quit. In reality, having their manager listen carefully to what they say will ignite their passion for the organization, and many people will become more serious. In any event, there are a certain number of people who will quit, and that's the way it is.

Let's assume there are two organizations with two different management styles. In one organization, managers, in general, are reluctant to listen to their employees because they are worried about losing some of the employees by listening to them too much. Thus, they continue doing their business as usual. In the other organization, managers face their employees openly and attentively listen to them expressing their true feelings and ideas. Which organization do you think will be more productive? With certainty I say, "it is the latter by a big margin."

## Team members actively participate in one-on-one meetings and grow

Once you see the direction in which your team member wants to go, you start to consider how it can be achieved. If what your team member is aiming for is something that can be done within your department, you can start figuring out how they can start getting there. For example, if a team member is interested in assisting with someone else's work, you can check if there is such an opportunity for them to do so. If a job opportunity is in another department, you can discuss the possibility of a transfer.

Another example in this case, you can say, "Let's discuss how you can be transferred to that division, this is in consideration of the future from a somewhat longer-term perspective. The opportunity may not come up right away, but it would be nice if you could participate in a cross-functional project, for example."

Or you can ask the person, "Do you know specifics about the work that you want to do?" The answer may reveal that he/she is still just dreaming about it without knowing much about the job. In such a case you can advise the person, "Why not meet with someone who oversees that job so you can find out more about what the job entails? It might enhance your sense of reality about it." After speaking with the person and having a sense of reality, he/she may think, "Yes, this is what I want to do," or "This may not be what I want." If the answer is negative, all he/she must do is to search again. If it is positive, you can support that person to move forward.

The feedforward meetings that I started with the members of my department turned out to be very enjoyable, both for me and for them. My team members actively participated in these one-on-one meetings. I will talk about the effects of these meetings in the next section. If I had focused the meetings on feedback, we would have felt uncomfortable for sure. My team members might have avoided these one-on-one meetings by giving excuses.

Although your work situation usually changes each month, the way you conduct feedforward meetings from the second session on, is basically the same. You focus on helping them find what they want. After several months of these meetings, when the team members set a clear direction, you will switch to a style in which you mostly talk about their day-to-day work while occasionally checking in on their direction.

Additionally, there is one more important point. It is a fact that the real power of feedforward meetings lies outside of the 30-minute monthly sessions. When feedforward meetings become a habit, even the daily communication between managers and team members becomes feedforwarding. It becomes normal for people to talk about the future. Once that happens, even if we face business difficulties, all members will be interested in how to overcome them and will naturally find solutions.

Feedforward communication does not stay only between managers and team members. It starts taking hold among the team members and becomes the norm among colleagues. The entire department is reborn as a team with one eye on the future.

# 3.
## Feedforward revitalizes both individuals and teams

---

### Individuals become happier and more active

When we started feedforward meetings and our daily communication progressed in the feedforwarding manner, the members' motivation was enhanced. The speed of the change was dependent on their original level of motivation, but everyone was headed in a positive direction.

First of all, each member became cheerful and lively as the team started looking toward the future. There is also another very important factor. The members realized that there was someone (the manager) who truly cared about them.

That's because we use the concept of *level of abstraction* when doing feedforward. (I'll talk more about the abstraction levels in Part II; so, please bear with me even if the concept is new to you). A higher level of abstraction means a higher point of view. You will be able to observe not only yourself but also others using this higher point of view. When you become considerate of others, your whole team's work improves as well. This is because you will aim to achieve not only your own goals but also the goals of those around you.

### Getting the job done faster with drastically reduced overtime

I provide here an example of a department for which I was appointed as manager. In that department, the work had always been hard, which resulted in overtime and long hours. Not surprisingly, the turnover rate was high. Half a year after introducing feedforward meetings to this department, it changed significantly and became the department with the least overtime work in the company.

When I first started working in this division, the members' monthly average overtime hours were more than 60 hours. It was a department that did not require them to work on weekends and holidays, but the daily workloads were very high. Some people had more than 80 hours of overtime each month, which was a big problem for the company.

I personally set a goal to reduce the average monthly overtime to less than 40 hours within six months. Our activities resulted in the average overtime being reduced to 35 hours. Even after my transfer to another department within a year, and to my delight, the overtime hours continued to decrease with the average falling to below 30 hours.

The main reason for this success was that feedforward thinking had become so natural to the team that their internal motivation of each team member remained high, and they continued to improve upon their work. One of our members said, "We used to work extremely hard when the deadline approached at the end of the month, the end of the quarter, and the end of the year. During those times, it was normal for us to leave work after 11:00 p.m. Now, I don't know why, but we all can go home by 8:00 pm at the latest."

They became more creative when reviewing their work. Conversely when they reviewed their work in a PDCA manner, they would spend a lot of time looking at the past, figuring out why they needed to work long hours and further spent time collecting information about the root cause. In the process of doing this they would dig up a lot of materials to reflect upon but wouldn't come up with many ideas for improvement. So much time and energy was spent on reflection that it took a long time before they could take any necessary action.

When they started to review their work with the feedforward mindset, they were able to generate one good idea after another. For example, all the members shared the vision of their future, "We can work efficiently and leave the office without overtime." To materialize it, they came up with creative and effective ideas one after another such as "Let's stop doing XX," "Let's reduce the frequency of YY from three to one per month," and "Let's change the procedure of ZZ."

From a cognitive science perspective, feedforward thinking results in the release of dopamine in the prefrontal cortex, which has the effect of allowing us to be more creative with our activities.

### Feedforward spread throughout the company

Changes in my team became noticeable throughout the company. Managers of other departments asked me, "Why is your team so lively and performing so well?" When I answered, "I'm doing feedforward," they started asking me, "Please teach my team, too." So, I set up a meeting with managers and spent about an hour explaining what I was doing. Essentially, what I shared was the same as what you are reading in this book.

First and foremost, I told them, "Feedforward is a time for each team member to discuss what they want to do, rather than having the manager give feedback on their work." Next, I talked about how to hold a briefing session and how to specifically conduct feedforward meetings. Some of these managers put it into practice, others didn't, and some couldn't manage the time though they wanted to.

Those managers who practiced it all felt that they were successful. After seeing their results, some other managers became interested in trying it. In some cases, team members in other departments learned about the benefits of feedforward and asked their managers to participate.

Furthermore, a project team that had improved its operations through feedforward won an internal contest, proving the effectiveness of feedforward. The team became the representative of the Japanese branch office and participated in the world competition where they gave a presentation.

The effects of Feedforward are summarized as follows:

In the process of looking to the future through Feedforward, you will be able to naturally discover your issues and work to improve them. Since the starting point is goal setting, you will tend to grow more self-reliant and motivated naturally.

In addition, since Feedforward is a simple technique that allows you to think and talk about the future, anyone can use it immediately. It's simple, yet highly effective, and can have a very fast and contagious positive impact on everyone.

# 4.

## Role of forwarder and receiver

### One forwarder and one receiver

You can Feedforward to anyone, anywhere, anytime.

Feedforward is effective not only in meetings between managers and team members but also in daily conversations including those between parents and children, as well as informal exchanges between teachers and students at school.

I see, all around me, many cases where everyday life can be described as being in the Feedforward field. Everyone who talks about the future and naturally starts moving toward it is causing its materialization. In the classes I teach at university, my students carry on conversations in which they ask each other questions such as, "What are you going to do next?" What makes *Feedforward* appealing is that it can be done easily.

First, let me touch upon the feedforward basics. The person who gives feedforward is called "*the feedforwarder or in short the forwarder*," and the person who receives it is "the receiver." The role is not fixed, and anyone can play either role depending on the situation. The forwarders care about the receivers' success and help them look to the future. It is also possible to feedforward onto yourself, in which case you are taking the role of both the forwarder and the receiver.

## A forwarder is always rooting for and supporting the receiver

A forwarder is someone who orients the receiver's conscious and subconscious toward the future. In the example I introduced earlier, I as the manager, was the forwarder and each of my team members was the receiver. The forwarder's role is to inspire the receivers to work toward the future.

The forwarder is the receiver's absolute ally and works together with the receiver to discover his/her future. It's as if the forwarder walks with the receiver in the dark, holding a flashlight in hand, and shining the light in front of the receiver. This helps the receiver move forward. Note, that the forwarder does not need to know the receiver's goal.

Feedforward is a practical and easy-to-use tool; you can feedforward even when the goal is not clear.

When a manager has an interview with a team member, an experienced manager may see what seems to be the member's goal during the conversation. However, know that the aim of feedforward is to encourage the receiver to be conscious of their future and discover the goal by themselves without the assistance of the forwarder pointing it out. This applies to the common situation where teachers talk to their students, or where parents talk to their children, pointing out a possible future for them.

In the past, it was possible for the managers to give their team members the goals they should achieve when they met together. This was because the managers generally had a clear goal for them. They also had a pretty good idea about what that person should do to achieve their goal.

However, in today's world, both the goal itself and the path to reach it are unclear and diverse. Although it may have always been that way, the degree of diversity in the world has increased exponentially, especially for the last 10 years or so. Which means it is very likely that the manager's ideas about their goals are wrong in the first place. Even in such circumstances, feedforward can work because *Feedforward* **is a technique for the receivers to find their own future.**

## Forwarders need to stay calm

What should the forwarders keep in mind? First, they need to think of the opportunity to Feedforward as an important time and a safe space. Each time forwarders and receivers share this feedforward opportunity, they do so as if it is *the first and last time.*

You can feedforward anywhere. You can do it during your lunch break at work, while you are having dinner with your family, or when you are having a dinner party with friends. Feedforward can be done at any time. However, I am mindful of seizing the moment as it may be a *one and only* chance, so when I ask, "What do you want to do next?" I am always prepared to give a worthy feedforward.

Before feedforwarding informally or formally, as with a meeting, you as a forwarder should do two things. One is to make up your mind as being absolutely on the receiver's side. Another is to believe in yourself by saying to yourself, "I can create the receiver's future by working together with him/her." and "I am capable of doing it."

Believing in yourself and the receiver will trigger the feedforward mechanism. I'll explain the reason why in Part II.

# 5.

## Three key questions in feedforwarding

---

### "How are you doing lately?"

When you perform feedforwarding, basically you can do so with three simple questions. First, forwarders break the ice when they meet with the receiver. An icebreaker is an introduction to make them relaxed.

After saying, "Thank you for your hard work the other day," or "Thank you for your help as always," engage in some informal dialogue to help the receiver relax. You don't have to spend much time on this. A couple of minutes would suffice.

So, you begin feedforwarding with your first question, "How are you doing lately?" Whether you are meeting for the first time or have already met several times, you can start with this question. Let the receiver say whatever he/she wants to say. There are many different answers to this question. Some people might talk about things that are going well, some people might talk about things that are not.

I intentionally avoid asking about the past. In many cases, some time has passed since the last meeting. If I say to the receiver, "Tell me about what happened since our last meeting," I will make the receiver become conscious of the past. So, I do not encourage their reflection of the past. Of course, some people might start talking about the past, but I never focus on it. The conversation around the first question, "How are you doing lately?" should usually take as little as 10-15 minutes. Then we move on to the second question.

### "What do you want to do from now on?" or "What are you going to do next?"

After spending some time on the first question, you then should ask the receiver the second question, "What are you going to do next?" This question will set the receiver's subconscious mind in motion. You listen to what the receiver wants to say about their future and accept it unequivocally by acknowledging using this phrase, "I see. That's great." This part of the conversation often lasts about 10 minutes. Then we move on to the third question.

### "What do you want to do further ahead?" "If you make it a little bigger, what will it look like?"

The third question is to help the receiver expand his/her thinking on the future in terms of time frame and scale. You can ask questions like, "What do you want to do further ahead?" and/or "If you make it a little bigger, what will it look like?" You will have the receiver look further into the future and scale up their thoughts. When you are dialoguing, it is important for you to look the receiver in the eye and to sincerely believe in the other person, *You can do it*, from the bottom of your heart.

Regarding these three questions, "How are you doing lately?" is a starting point and "What do you want to do from now on?" is a future point. These two questions, and their answers, formulate a gap. If we don't create this gap, our brain won't be generating enough energy to make something great happen, as it perceives no change is necessary.

Well, what do you think? Feedforward is something that you can easily practice with the three key questions listed above. Thanks to forwarders, receivers will become conscious of the future, work on the future, and naturally get results which will make them feel happy.

### A case example of asking the three key questions

Let's take a look at a successful case of feedforward using these three key questions.

At a dinner party, a 65-year-old business owner sat next to me. He is a successful man who runs a famous shop in the Kyushu region in Japan. He read my book and said, "I came here to ask for your advice."

He is the fourth generation carrying the company that has been in business for nearly 100 years but seemed somewhat unmotivated and unsure. During dinner, I at times, gave him a feedforward. Of course, I wouldn't say "I will feedforward you," or "We will start a feedforward session."

After a quick introduction, the atmosphere between us became relaxed. So, I asked him, "How are things for you these days?" and listened to what he wanted to share with me. While I was listening, I nodded and responded to each of his statements saying, "Is that right?" or "That's great!" When he told me something negative, I acknowledged it **as something that had happened in the past,** commenting "That **must have been** very difficult." Then I continued the conversation with a future-oriented way.

I asked, "What would you like to do from here on out?" He replied, "I want to become the number one shop in the Kyushu area."

"That's great. Then what would you like to do after

that?" I continued. I took the liberty to inflate his story in my head and said, "What do you think about becoming number one in Western Japan?" Then I added, "Would it be possible for you to extend the area to include Eastern Japan as well?"

He smiled while we were having the conversation and said, "While I am talking with you, I feel it is getting clearer about what I should do. Thank you so much for your advice today!" Then he went home.

As you can see in the above example, *Feedforward* can be practiced casually in daily life, without preparing yourself with something special or any agenda.

# 6.

## Forwarders' important power to listen

### Big ears, small mouth, and gentle eyes

Effective forwarders are those who possess a pure interest in and a supportive attitude toward the receivers' success. It is essential for the forwarders to listen to what the other person has to say until the end.

The important quality of listening is to remain attentive with your mind focused on the speaker. It is critical that you not only hear, but that you listen with care. While you are listening carefully, you will inevitably have some impressions or questions. However, it is recommended that you stay focused on the receiver and contribute to the conversation by saying simple things like, "Is that right? If so, what would you like to do?"

When you are at work, you tend to have *a big mouth, small ears, and hard-looking eyes.* A big mouth here refers to expressing your opinions, small ears to hardly listening to others' opinions, and hard-looking eyes to critically finding the others' shortcomings and failures.

However, what we need for Feedforward is *big ears, small mouth, and gentle eyes." Big ears* here refer to attentive listening, *small mouth* to limiting yourself to speak only what is necessary, and *gentle eyes* to seeing the other's future.

## Don't listen to complaints too much

There is one thing you want to keep in mind when listening. While it is important to listen to the receiver attentively, you need to be aware of how you listen. For example, you may ask "Do you need any help?"

For team members, co-workers, lovers, and spouses, this question may be fairly common in day-to-day communications. Some people think that such a question is the first step to building a good relationship. However, your brain may start searching for problems when being asked, "Do you need any help?" Consequently, your brain focuses on the matters needing help and inhibits other activities.

There may be a situation where a person is complaining about something and you – as the forwarder – may nod and say, "Yes, yes, I understand. Then what happened?" Everyone has worries and uncertainties. When we express them, these feelings are amplified. If we continue to speak when asked further questions about our concerns, we may speak more than we intended to, and may end up regretting what we reveal, later thinking "I didn't mean to say that much."

What we talked about may have been the things that we were *not so sure about* or the things that we just *casually mentioned*. In either case, once the words come out from our mouth, they strengthen the circuit inside of our brain. Therefore, it is not always helpful to dig deeper and listen to the other person. If you notice that the person is focusing more on complaints or negative words than when you started conversation, it is prudent for you to stop and change the topic. It is often the case that doing so is better for the other person.

## Why listen?

There are various intentions behind the listening process. For example,

- To get along with the person (to be liked)
- To solve the problem for that person
- To solve the issues between that person and yourself
- To solve the problem between the person and the company

The lowest level among the above is "listening to be liked." For example, the situation may be where you respond like a servant to a high-ranking manager saying, "Very well.

You are right. That's impressive!" This may be done even though you don't have much interest in that person. This is the state of listening to the other person comes from your own motive to improve your position by becoming the manager's favorite.

What you want to keep in mind is to listen "for the sake of the other person." If you have this perspective in mind, you will know when you need to make decisions such as **"I shouldn't ask anything more questions."**

# 7.

## Feedforward requires the power to wait – Patience

---

### Wait a little while before asking, "What would you like to do from now on?"

Due to the nature of my work, my clients as well as my friends often send me e-mails and messages asking for my advice.

Sometimes the message is lengthy, but I carefully read it first and reply "Oh is that so? It must have been difficult." and wait for a while. Then, after about half a day, I send a message asking, "What would you like to do from now on?" to get them looking to the future. I don't dig in deeper, nor ask any further questions on those issues in which they contacted me for advice.

When I send a message saying, "Oh is that so? It must have been difficult," their brain and mind begin to sort things out. Then, they are able to review what they wrote about, and formulate a position about where they stand from a slightly higher perspective. With this process they may start feeling that it's not such a big deal or that they can manage it. Thus, they calm down.

With this timing, they receive a message from me, "What would you like to do from now on?" By then, their brain has organized the information. They are naturally looking forward, and they feel like talking about their future and goals.

This process is not limited to emails and communications on social media. When you observe the other persons' situation and feel that they are amid chaos, it is better to stay quiet and wait for a while. Then, when the confusion has been sorted out, you can ask *what they want to do from now on*. They will then begin their conversation with something like, "Well, I thought about it."

They may continue talking about the past or present issues or complaints in response to your question, "What would you like to do from now and into the future?" It indicates that they haven't sorted things out yet. In such a case, it is advisable to wait a little longer.

The premise here is that the brain takes a certain amount of time to organize various pieces of information, and this can only be done at the individual's own pace.

## Digging into the past is risky

By listening you become responsible to the other person. It's irresponsible for you to just listen and do nothing. It's also risky for the person who spoke to you. Avoid the situation which obligates you to the person because you heard too much. It's better that you change the conversation at some point and start talking about the future for both of you to be happy.

There is a style of treatment that aims to improve the situation by digging into the past of the person who is suffering. Suffering such as trauma, understanding what happened, understanding the cause, etc., and forgiving oneself and others. It is true that there are people who find the cause of their trauma by digging into their past, and resolving it to become better, but these people are rare indeed.

In most cases, multiple causes are intertwined to cause the effects in your life and these causes cannot be easily disentangled. Even if you're lucky enough to find some causes and try to untangle them, it is usually temporary, and the pattern formed in your brain becomes so strong that it's easy to return to it.

From the cognitive science point of view, the act of digging into the past and looking for trauma is equivalent to re-living it. It is like having the same experience by sending electrical signals to the brain's *bad memory circuit*. For example, if you remember about being bullied in the past, the reaction in your brain and body is the same as though you are being bullied twice. If you repeat it, it is natural that your mental state and even your physical state will get worse.

## Memories are rebuilt by looking to the future

So instead of digging into the past, look to the future. When we look to the future, information from the past is automatically rearranged and reconstructed in our brains. Information about the past is arranged (conveniently in a sense) in a way that it fits into the desired future. Even if there was a difficult event in the past, the memory of *I'm glad I went through that hardship at the time* is built, which will strengthen your ability to face the future happily. The events that happened may not change, but you can make your own interpretation of the events. Don't leave that interpretation to someone else.

I have a friend who lost his parents when he was young. He overcame hardships to become a successful businessman. Referring to his past, he says, "It was really tough at that time. But because my parents passed away early on, I was able to undergo unique and various life experiences from the time of their death, which led to where I am today." The painful memories of the past are rebuilt in the brain as valuable events.

In this example, the brain reorganized the past memories to fit to the current state. Feedforward takes you one step further. Not only does it accelerate the process of rebuilding past memories, but it also begins creating *future memories*. A *future memory* may be an unfamiliar term, but it is a concept that is commonly used in the world of cognitive science. It is said that the brain cannot distinguish between what actually happened and what is imagined.

For example, imagine a situation where an event occurred, although it *has not actually happened yet*. If the image is clear enough and the sense of reality is elevated enough, our brain will perceive it as if it *actually happened*. Even though it comes from an imagined future, it feels to the brain like a *memory*, as if it has already happened. Then, the brain begins to organize and rebuild past memories in line with those *future memories*. As a result, even if you have painful memories, you will be able to feel that it was a necessary experience for your bright future.

## It's taboo to say "you said XYZ before"

I have a feedforward session with my clients about once a month. Often, what the receiver says is different from the last time. This is because goals are often updated, and they talk about things on a much bigger scale.

At that time, I don't say, "You said *this...*, last month." If I go out of my way to remind them about what was previously said, the receiver's brain will go back to the state a month ago. This would ruin the progress made during the past month. The circuits of the brain (one month ago) would have been intentionally stimulated by the receiver. Reminding them of what they said one month ago is like returning the receiver's attention to the previous months' thoughts. The only reason this would make sense is if the situation is bad now and it was great before, otherwise you don't need to bother going back to reference the past.

It is common for a manager or a teacher to say something like, "You set these goals, but four out of five have not been achieved." Meetings like this are common between managers and team members, teachers and students, etc. If the person has completely forgotten the fact that he/she couldn't achieve them, such a statement may be necessary. However, if the person is properly aware of it, there is no value from the cognitive science viewpoint in emphasizing such a fact.

## When you are asked for advice

During feedforwarding, you may be asked for specific advice regarding the receiver's goal. For example, let's assume the person says, "I have a project that I want to develop overseas, so I want to improve my English. What should I do?"

At this time, I simply ask, "Well, how are you planning to do it?"

"I'm thinking I should start building my vocabulary."

Then I answer affirmatively, "I see. That sounds good."

And I will add, "Please keep looking for a method that suits you."

The point here is to basically affirm whatever the receiver says. Naturally, we need to respect whatever method the receivers share with us, as it is something they came up with at the moment their goal or target was set. After that, we encourage them to keep thinking of various ways without being bound by their current idea.

As you set a goal or a target, your brain will find the best way possible on how to accomplish it with the information it has at the time. Also, *the best way* is constantly changing as the situation changes. Various ideas come to mind every day through your subconscious. This is like an adjustment as I explained in the section of FFA in Chapter 2, Short-term Future-oriented Planning: Target Setting ➡ Subconscious Adjustment ➡ Action. So, it is beneficial for you to incorporate many new ideas.

A forwarder is a guide for the receiver. You can suggest options to select from but be extra careful not to impose any of your own ideas.

# 8.

## Feedforward works for any learning style

---

### Three styles of learning

Our learning styles are divided into the following three types:

Action-oriented: Wanting to act right away.

Analysis-oriented: Wanting to know everything before taking action.

Replication-oriented: Wanting to follow in someone else's footsteps, as it is faster.

Let's suppose you bought a digital camera. What would you do first? If you turn on the power and start taking pictures, then you should classify yourself as an *action-oriented person*. If you carefully read the instruction manual before starting to use the camera, you are an *analysis-oriented person*. Finally, if you ask someone who knows it well for hints on how to use the camera, even before the use of the camera on your own, then you are *replication-oriented person*.

Regardless of what type of person you are, you may start in the manner consistent with one style but then something happens, and you don't understand what to do next. You might then adopt another style. As an example, you may have jumped into using the camera, but now you read the instruction manual. If it is the case, you have a hybrid type of learning style – one that is both, *action-oriented and analysis-oriented*. Generally, each person knows which learning type they are.

## Communicate differently depending on the learning style

If you know the other person's strongest pattern of these 3 types, you can carry out your work more effectively.

For example, there is a new member who has just been assigned to your sales department. An action-oriented manager may tell that person, "Just try calling the client."

If the new team member is analysis-oriented, they may think "I can't call because I don't have enough knowledge about our products." Analysis-oriented people can't take action until they learn about how the product functions. However, it would be very difficult for a new employee who has just joined the company to say to the manager, "I can't make a call because I don't know much about the product yet." In such a situation, if the manager pushes his style and says, "You don't have to understand, just call and make an appointment. Learn the work by doing it," this new employee may not be able to continue in this job.

On the other hand, action-oriented new employees who don't know anything about the product will just make an appointment and ask a more experienced colleague, "Please come with me to the appointment." Whereas, replication-oriented new employees will say, "Let me go with you. I'll observe and learn."

### How to support different learning types

*Analysis-oriented* types tend to hate making mistakes and dislike experiencing failures. So, it is necessary to allow them enough time to learn. They will also benefit from a role-playing method and having them review what they need to learn from various perspectives. They do better by being given the opportunity to learn until they are satisfied and not being interfered with too much during that stage in their learning process. They grow step by step.

*Action-oriented types* will thrive when you encourage and support their actions by saying, "Feel free to try what you think is needed," or "Try them all until you are satisfied." They tend not to listen to other's advice, and they like to try, see, and learn things on their own. What you really need to teach them is what they absolutely shouldn't be doing. They will grow while making moderate-scale mistakes. They are good at sprinting. What you want to do is to keep their momentum going.

*Replication-oriented types* want to learn the whole process. So, it is beneficial to give them the opportunity to get the big picture as early as possible. Also, they are more likely to grow if they have a chance to carefully observe the work of others who perform it well. They are often not so good at breaking down work and learning it piece by piece. They need to be taught the relationship between each of the parts and the whole.

Looking from the outside, action-oriented people give us good first impressions and tend to get good appraisals. Because what they do is notable, they appear to be doing it with enthusiasm and they perform massive actions, so they get results much faster.

Analysis-oriented people are slow starters, so they won't get the same results out of their work at first. However, as they steadily gain strength, they may catch up and eventually surpass others in their work performance.

The hybrid type of *replication-oriented and action-oriented* will grow quickly at the beginning. On the other hand, the hybrid type of people who are *replication-oriented and analysis-oriented* take time to grow. In either hybrid type, they are good at grasping the whole picture. Once they get going, they will become highly reliable people as they can play an active role with a broad perspective.

You need to be careful if your learning type as a manager is different from that of a team member. You must be mindful not to force your style. If you're an action-oriented type, you may feel that the other person should just try it. However, if the person is an analysis-oriented person, you need to help him/her learn the work first. Or, if you find that your team member is replication-oriented, you should think of a plan, such as adding more time for the person to accompany senior members.

Managers tend to push their way of doing things, but the best way is to let the other person choose their preferred way.

## You will learn with more experience

Even if you feel that you are an action-oriented type – as you continue working over time, you may realize that the work progresses faster if you understand the whole process (replication-oriented). Thus, you begin developing a better way to do your work.

Taking cooking as an example. There are people who follow the recipe (analysis-oriented), people who try to make it once on their own (action-oriented), and people who want someone to teach them (replication-oriented).

People who are analysis-oriented may cook carefully for the first time, but as they learn how to cook over time, they begin to come up with their own ideas even for a first-time recipe. They may think, "It is quicker to do it this way while following the recipe, or it is easier for me to do it this way (action-oriented) even though the book says this," and so on.

It is common to acquire the ability to apply different skills while gaining various experiences. Each person has a style that is easy to apply for them. It is a good idea to be conscious of each person's learning style when communicating with them, not only during meetings between managers and team members but also when interacting with people in general.

An advantage of feedforward is that it works regardless of the receiver's learning style. You can use the same approach for everyone because all we are concerned with, when using feedforward, is to have them look toward the future. Regardless of their learning types, people will take actions accordingly with their own learning style after looking at their future.

# PART II

# The Path to Become an Advanced Feedforwarder

In Part II, I discuss the concepts and techniques to become an advanced *Feedforwarder* (or *forwarder* for short). For Feedforward, all you have to do is focus on the future and work on it. But to conduct more advanced and effective Feedforward, forwarders want to be conscious of three points: *Increase the receiver's level of abstraction*, *Increase the receiver's self-efficacy*, and *Help the receiver set goals*. By being aware of these, you will be able to do better feedforward.

CHAPTER 4

# Increase the Receiver's Level of Abstraction

## 1.

### The higher the level of abstraction, the broader the field of vision

**See one's position from a higher point of view**

What are the levels of abstraction? Imagine a big circle. Let's call this circle *newspaper*. Inside this circle are various newspapers. Here, the circle is the *set*, and each newspaper inside is an *element* of the set.

To be more specific, the set of newspapers might include *Japan Times, Washington Post, New York Times, Wall Street Journal,* etc. In this case, the set we are calling *Newspaper* has a higher abstraction level than the specific brands of newspapers within this set. The named newspapers in the lower level of abstraction are wrapped in the concept of higher level of abstraction called *Newspaper.*

Raising the level of abstraction is like riding in a helicopter and looking at the scenery below from a higher point of view. When you were on the ground, you could only see your surroundings. However, as the helicopter goes up and up into the air, you would see that the place you were is known as Town A for example. If it rises further, you will recognize the place is in County B and State C. Your perception changes as does your field of view, as you go higher and higher.

Another example may be easier to understand. If you are in your office holding a *black ballpoint pen*, there are different levels of abstraction above it such as *ballpoint pen*s then, *writing instruments*, and then, *office supplies*. On the same level of the *black ballpoint pen*s, there are *blue ballpoint pens* and *red ballpoint pens* as shown in the diagram below.

When feedforwarding, if the forwarder can be aware of the receiver's current abstraction level, the effect of feedforward will greatly increase. It's not that feedforward can't be performed if the level of abstraction stays the same. However, if the receiver's level of abstraction goes up, his/ her state improves. A higher level of abstraction widens one's view and helps the receiver to see the future more clearly.

## What is the Levels of Abstraction?

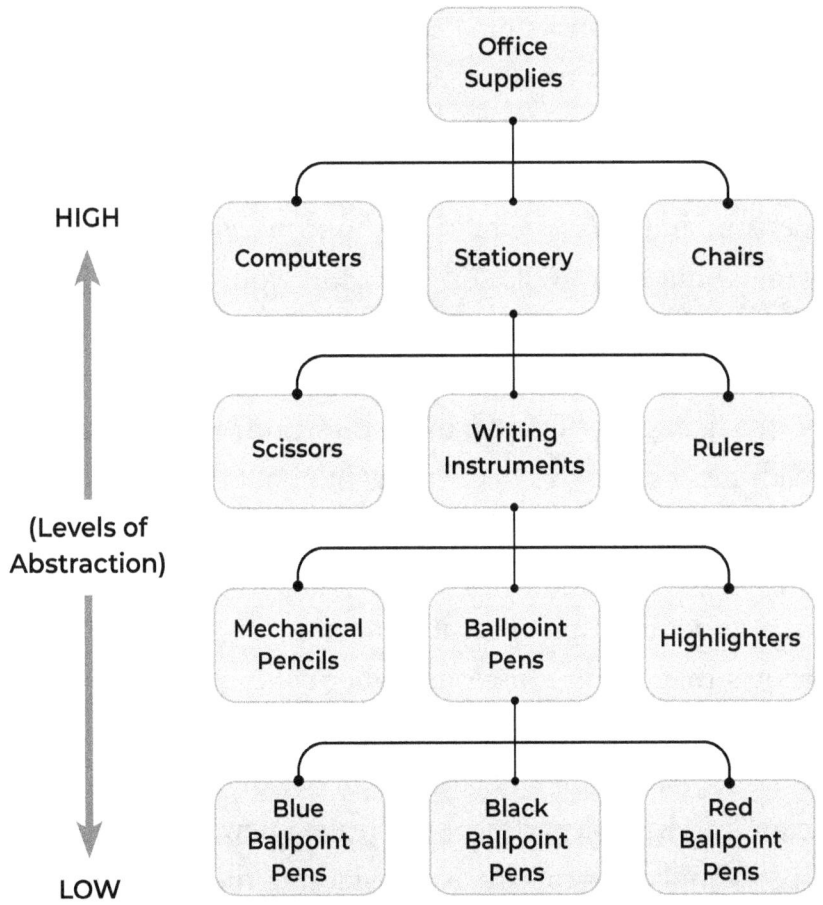

## Determine the abstraction level of the receiver

Feedforwarders talk about the future while sensing the receiver's level of abstraction. It is not necessary to know precisely where the receiver's level of abstraction is. The forwarder needs to think about how the receiver perceives the world with respect to a certain theme.

How much you think about people other than yourself is one indicator that can give insight into understanding your level of abstraction. People who are self-absorbed have a low level of abstraction. As they start thinking about their surroundings, their abstraction level naturally increases.

For example, let's say you're feedforwarding to a salesperson, and he/she is talking about *my job*. At that time, you would ask, "What do you think your team should do to move forward?" The response to this question will give you a rough idea of the person's level of abstraction.

If Mr. A says, "Do you mean our team? I've been so busy with myself that I've never thought about that before," this clearly indicates that his level of abstraction is low. On the other hand, if Ms. B replies, "My team members are working in a good atmosphere as it relates to this new project," it shows that she is conscious of her colleagues as well. Her abstraction level is higher than that of Mr. A's. In addition, if Mr. C says, "I would like to have a regular meeting with the manufacturing department to create a new project," his response indicates that he is considering the manufacturing department as part of the team, even though he is in the sales department. Therefore, his level of abstraction is even higher.

## Raising the level of abstraction with feedforward

During your feedforward communications, you could also do something like this: Let's suppose a subordinate says to you, "I came up with a new project idea."

As the boss, you might respond, "That's very good! How can we use this plan to change the entire department?" This is a question that invites the receiver – your subordinate – to become conscious of a higher level of abstraction. If your subordinate responds positively, you can carry on with your dialogue by saying, "That sounds great! What would you need to propose this project to influence the entire company? Why don't we think about it together?" This communication makes the receiver aware of raising the level of abstraction further still.

Feedforward is a technique that encourages the receiver's thinking to face the future. In doing so, it supports the receiver as they climb up the pyramid regarding the levels of abstraction. Specifically, it is desirable to do feedforwarding so that the receiver can move up one level of abstraction from their current level. This is a powerful technique that quickly raises the receiver's point of view and level of abstraction.

You may have heard successful business owners share their experiences. For example, let's say that these entrepreneurs were talking about going marlin fishing on a yacht over this coming weekend. Some of you might think, "They are boasting," but that may not be necessarily the case.

There is a possibility that they are talking about a higher

level of abstraction to the young people for whom they have high hopes. Just listening to stories about their world – a world which you have never imagined – can lift your perspective. And then if the person says, "Let's go marlin fishing on my yacht, just you and me next time," it becomes a feedforward communication to you as a receiver. When feedforwarding is done – at one level higher of abstraction – as compared to the level you are currently situated at – it will greatly enhance your sense of reality about the future.

In the same way as in the above example, the forwarder speaks to the receiver with words and questions that are aimed at the level of abstraction one level higher than where the receiver is. When the receiver can feel the reality of the world in the elevated level of abstraction, his/her level of abstraction will move up by one step as well.

# 2.

## The Receiver's level of abstraction

---

### What is the receiver's level of abstraction?

Let's summarize the level of abstraction for clarity. The diagram shown below represents the guidelines for the level of abstraction. An advanced forwarder can determine the receiver's current level and raise it to the next level. Let's check them one by one.

| Level 0 | **Chaos:** Not knowing what to do. |
|---|---|
| Level 1 | **Status quo:** Accepting and maintaining the status quo is the goal. |
| Level 2 | **Learning/improving:** Become aware of the methods and techniques to achieve goals outside the status quo and start learning them. |
| Level 3 | **Understanding/applying:** Clearly understand the methods and techniques to achieve goals and make use of them for oneself. |
| Level 4 | **Abstraction + Comprehension of specialized fields:** Begin to understand that it is possible to view the entire universe consistently and hierarchically and apply the knowledge to one's field of expertise. |
| Level 5 | **Abstraction of the whole universe + Application to each field:** Possess the level of abstraction that comprehends the entire universe consistently and hierarchically and apply the knowledge to the multiple fields. |
| Level 6 | Discovery and development of new rules. |

Feedforward is especially needed for those receivers who are at Levels 0 to 3. More specifically they are as follows:

| | |
|---|---|
| **Level 0** | **Chaos:** They don't know about their goal. They don't know what is needed to achieve the goal. |
| **Level 1** | **Status quo:** While being compromised and giving in, they feel they are okay where they are at the moment. |
| **Level 2** | **Learning/improving:** They have begun understanding there is a better way and they start learning how to achieve goals. |
| **Level 3** | **Understanding/applying:** They are using what they learned. They are finding their way, and they can practice their knowledge. |

The forwarder first assesses the receivers' current level. If the receivers are in the *chaos* stage (Level 0), the forwarder helps them become aware that a higher abstract world exists and calms their confusion in the chaos. If the receivers are in the *learning/improving* stage (Level 2), the forwarder guides the receivers to apply their knowledge properly. In this manner, the forwarder helps the receivers increase their level one step at a time.

# Information Hierarchy Pyramid

The world we see is different depending
on the level of abstraction we are at.

**Level 6**   **Discovery and development of new rules**

**Level 5**   **Abstraction of the Whole Universe + Application to
Each Field:**
Possess the level of abstraction that comprehend the
entire universe consistently and hierarchically and apply
the knowledge to the multiple fields.

**Level 4**   **Abstraction + Comprehension of specialized fields:**
Begin to understand that it is possible to view the entire
universe consistently and hierarchically and apply the
knowledge to one's field of expertise.

**Level 3**   **Understanding / Applying:**
Clearly understand the methods and techniques to
achieve goals and make use of them for oneself.

**Level 2**   **Learning / Improving:**
Become aware of the methods and techniques to achieve
goals outside the status quo and start learning them.

**Level 1**   **Status quo:**
Accepting and maintaining the status quo is the goal.

**Level 0**   **Chaos:** Not knowing what to do.

An advanced feedforwarder listens to what the receiver is saying, understands the level in which the receiver resides, and raises him/her to the next level.

The pyramid of abstraction introduced on the previous page can be stratified for each item that a person considers important, such as work, hobbies, health, family, etc. Thus, it does not show uniformly where the person belongs within the hierarchy. For example, I'm at a high level of the pyramid when it comes to feedforward, but if I'm assigned to bake a cake for my family, I'm at Level 0, chaos, as I don't know what to do. Please understand that this is a hierarchy of abstraction levels to be considered for each specific field.

### Judging the state of the receiver with the five senses

In order to determine the receiver's level of abstraction, the forwarder not only listens to the words spoken by the receiver but also feels the other person's state using all of their five senses. This process is what I refer to as "observation."

While carrying on conversations, you as the forwarder, observe the receiver and feel the indications as to where he/she is at. You can ask questions, such as: Is the receiver getting the point? The receiver is replying or nodding, but is he/she really understanding what you are communicating? Is this person's body positioning in a leaning forward position? Is there a *sparkle* in their eyes indicating their interest? Your efforts won't be effective if you blindly speak only from a high level of abstraction. You need to observe the receivers with your five senses and assess what level of abstraction they are in before talking about the future. This requires a further explanation.

Here is an example. There was a man who was 34 years old and wanted to start a new business. He was working in a technical field, however he decided to start a business within 6 months.

I had a feedforward session with him. First, I needed to grasp his level of abstraction. I knew in advance that he had an elevated level of skills and experiences in his specialized field. However, in terms of entrepreneurship, I wanted to ask some questions to understand what level of abstraction he was in.

"Do you know how much sales revenue you need to generate each month?"

"I have a rough idea."

"How many customers do you need for that?"

"I am calculating it now."

I continued my questions such as "Who do you want to target?" and "What are the possible business risks?" Through dialoging, I realized that he was not sufficiently ready to start his own business.

On the other hand, the answer to the question "What would make you happy?" was relatively clear. He had a clear image of his goal and was focused on it. This is especially important when owning your own business. Nevertheless, it revealed that he was not clear about the process leading up to his goal and what he needed to do from tomorrow on.

So, I asked more questions.

"Have you ever made a business plan?"

"No, I have not."

"I see. How do you think you can learn how to make a business plan?"

"Learn from seminars and books?"

"Sure, why don't you buy a couple of books and read them first?"

In this way, after my discovery process, I was able to provide him with specific advice at the end.

## People will grow because you truly care about them

Let's think about the essence of how people's minds (brain and heart) change.

When assessing the receivers' current situation and inviting them to the next level, the forwarder should *not* think of oneself at all. Feedforward is more effective if you do it solely for the sake of the other person. If you get even a little bit of your own ego involved, the other person's subconscious will notice it and will not be able to open up and climb the ladder of abstraction. It is a necessary condition that the forwarder is absolutely on the receiver's side.

The receiver entrusts everything to the forwarder. The receivers speak everything about themselves. The forwarder accepts what the receiver says in its entirety. If the forwarder puts his/her own interest in there, trust won't be established. Thinking of others from the bottom of your heart will create the condition to change their mind.

## Systems needed for future organizations

This is a story about the delegation of authority within an organization.

In order to delegate authority with peace of mind, it is necessary to believe that the person to whom you are delegating authority will do the job properly. If you have an unreliable subordinate, you will think that it would be easier and safer for you to do the task yourself, so it is difficult to entrust them with the job.

It would be ideal if your subordinates were better than you are (at least in some areas). Then you would truly feel secure in entrusting work to them. Before actively delegating authority, it is necessary to thoroughly nurture subordinates and/or hire excellent employees.

On the one hand it's a scary thing, because it is possible for your subordinates, when fully developed, to overtake your job and you might end up losing your position with the company. When this fear prevails within an organization, bosses will stop hiring strong candidates or stop fostering strong employees.

This phenomenon can also happen in parent-child relationships. When parents subconsciously don't want their children to surpass their own level of achievement, they interrupt their children's dreams and put a lid on their growth.

What we need is a system in which the supervisor who hires and trains subordinates, where the subordinates eventually surpass them, is highly regarded and highly evaluated in the company. Then, the supervisors can feel secure and work to develop their subordinates even to the point where they surpass the supervisors themselves.

Let's consider two cases. In one case, people say, "That department is amazing, because Manager A has achieved great results and is leading the way." In the other case, they say, "Manager B is great in facilitation and his department is amazing, mostly because he has created an excellent team and is producing results." For a future-oriented organization, it is necessary to have a personnel system where Manager B, in the latter case, is evaluated higher than Manager A in the former case.

I have heard that in Silicon Valley, people who can hire those who are better than themselves tend to be highly valued. Also, Japanese IT companies are gradually becoming like that. I believe this is an especially important way for an organization to continue to get good results. After all, organizations are made up of people.

# 3.

## Seeing a common future for organizations and individuals

### Organizations respect individual goals and individuals respect organizational goals

Every organization has goals. Individuals also have goals. If the goals of the organization and the goals of the individuals are aligned, then the more you work hard, the bigger your contribution to the organization will be, and you will be able to get closer to your dreams.

However, in reality, it is a common sentiment that personal dreams and company work are two separate things. The number of people who do not seek self-actualization within their company is increasing. At times like this, it is more important to find a "common future" where the goals of the organization and the goals of individuals overlap, even if only just a little.

For example, you consider your triathlon training and competitions to be more important than anything else. Your work may be just a means to earn money to participate in triathlons. That's fine. In any case, the work should be done properly during the scheduled work week. You are free to use your time outside of work however you like. Still, your interest and the organization's interest are overlapping as the organization wants you to apply yourself effectively during working hours, and you also want to work so you can earn money for your important hobby.

Nonetheless, even those who find themselves in an example similar to the above example, have a desire to contribute to the company. Otherwise, they would have left the company. When the organization respects the goals of the individual, and the individual respects the goals of the organization, each of us envisions a common future in which we are both successful. When we are moving toward this shared future together, we are in a balanced relationship.

## Understanding people's goals through regular communication

If an organization has ten employees, these individuals will have ten different futures. Of course, the common futures of the individuals and the organizations will also be ten. For an organization with one hundred employees, you will need one hundred common futures, and if you have one thousand, you will need one thousand common futures. To find a common future, we use the concept of *the levels of abstraction*. The higher the abstraction level, the easier it is to draw a common future.

If the manager knows what the team members are interested in and are aiming for, then he/she might be able to communicate with them more specifically. For example, at a one-on-one meeting, the manager says, "You said that you wanted to make use of your ability in skill ABC. There seems to be an opportunity for you to use your knowledge and skills in this new project."

The top of the company needs to set a high goal and always leads its employees. Meanwhile, the company managers observe the goals of their subordinates and find the common points to share between the company and the individuals.

---

## An organization and an individual share a goal at a certain level of abstraction

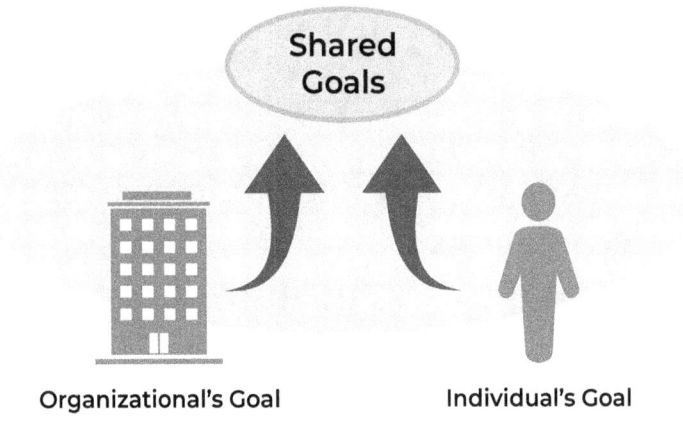

Organizational's Goal                    Individual's Goal

- Both the organization and the individuals have their balance wheel.

- Create a ( Shared Goals ) for each member of the organization.

- ( Shared Goals ) are created through feedforwarding between an immediate supervisor and an employee.

- Top management sets and maintains very high goals.

This is how organizations and individuals see a common future together. If you can use it well, the company and individual employees will come together and proceed toward the future. A partial overlap between the shared future of the company and the individual is enough. Individuals don't have to devote themselves entirely to the company.

Let's suppose an employee's goal is bigger and more attractive than the company's goal. If the company listens to that person and says, "Let's go with that," it's a pretty wise company. It is admirable for the top management to possess such wisdom to be able to adopt the employees' amazing goals and integrate those within the company.

# 4.

## The key to communication, between generations with different values, is the levels of abstraction

### Feedforward to bridge the generation gap

Especially in today's society, people have different values. In addition to personal values, there are values cultivated by the background of the times. These values may include values from the post-WW II era, the post-bubble-economy, and the millennial generation. Since each has a different set of values, it seems that they sometimes feel of uneasiness during the communication process, because they don't understand each other so well.

Let's say company members are between the ages of 18 and 65. The demographic, therefore, is that in 2018, the 18-year-olds were born in 2000, and 65-year-olds were born in 1953. Since there is a difference of up to 47 years from the year of birth, the state of society and experiences during that time will have been vastly different, so it is natural that the sense of values would also be dissimilar.

People in their 50s and 60s lived in a post-WWII era during which working hard was deemed important. In Japan, this same generation also enjoyed the bubble economy during the latter half of 1980s. After that, during the period of the last 20 years, a generation emerged that embodied diversity by experiencing an employment "ice age" and sharing household chores with both working spouses. In addition, there is the millennial generation.[2]

Thus, an organization will have people of various generations with differing values. Generally, it's hard to find a way to communicate well with people of all generations. However, feedforward can work effectively in communicating with people of all generations and all values.

## Unless they are convinced, they don't take action

Here, as an example, I will talk about communication with the millennial generation of Japan, which many people seem to feel is difficult.

---

2 In Japan it is referred to *Yutori generation* because people in this generation went through *Yutori* (pressure-free) education based on the government's revised guidelines started implementation in 2002.

With the change going to a *Yutori* (pressure-free) education, Japan has broken away from the overemphasis on knowledge and established a curriculum that emphasizes fostering the ability to think. Other major reforms were also carried out. These included the establishment of a new integrated learning and the emphasis on experiments, observations, surveys, research, presentations, and discussions to foster experiences and real feelings.

This generation has a completely different set of values than the older generations. Generally, they want to be role models. They want to be praised and want to work together with their peers. Also, they are self-aware and assert that they are the generation that does not need to be equipped with understanding the basics. Thus, they think that it is natural to expect someone to teach them. Basically, this generation has been given almost everything. Therefore, they think that if they don't understand something, it's because they haven't been taught, and they assertively say, "I don't know it at all." They don't like being given instructions. They are more inclined to wait for instructions, but when given instructions, they tend to show resistance.

This generation is also hesitant to take action if they don't understand the meaning behind the action they are about to take. They have a strong tendency to seek a fundamental understanding before engaging in any activity. I've heard a story about a baseball coach who said, "If they don't agree with my advice, they won't make a move." With the slightly older generations, there are situations where it is possible to say, "Just give it a try, and you'll see things more clearly as you go along." However, this generation requires agreement before they can act.

## A generation that has been praised

The millennial generation or *Yutori* generation in Japan has generally been praised and received approval throughout all aspects of their lives. They feel a sense of unease when they are not praised. They have been praised and received approval, but in many cases, it was not based on specific accomplishments but rather a general sense of approval. As a result, many of them, now adults, find themselves in a state of wanting recognition but not knowing exactly what they want to be recognized for. It can be described as an unending need for approval where they desire recognition without a clear direction of where they are heading.

In terms of generational comparison, their self-evaluation is relatively high. However, this self-evaluation is not based on striving toward a defined goal but rather on a sense of confidence derived from being somehow praised in the past. As a result, their ability to move forward is not particularly strong. When interacting with individuals from this generation, it is important to assist them in setting their own goals.

I'd like to share an episode I heard about a new employee from the millennial generation. He was working at a company where a client requested him to be removed from his assignment with them. One senior staff member was concerned and thought the new employee might be feeling down about this situation. The staff member approached him to offer some comforting words, saying that it could also be a matter of compatibility with this client.

To the senior staff member's surprise, the new employee responded by saying, "That's right, it's an issue of compatibility." The senior staff member was taken aback. He had imagined the new employee would express his frustration over his own shortcomings. The senior staff member was astonished beyond words. He couldn't even tell the new employee what he truly wanted to covey, "No, that's not what I really meant. There might have been some areas where you could have improved." Unfortunately, instead of reflecting on his actions that had angered the client, this new employee took the senior staff member's comforting words literally to heart. He concluded it was not his fault and it was a compatibility issue.

Furthermore, I heard the new employee go on to say, "I believe that removing myself would actually improve the team's performance, so it's for the greater good." The senior staff member was at a loss for words again because the new employee's statement sounded like it was someone else's problem to deal with. He seemed to treat the situation as if it didn't concern him personally. If the senior staff member had been familiar with the concept of *Feedforward*, it might have been possible that the situation could have had a better outcome.

Feedforward would approach this kind of situation first with consideration going to the goals of the client, the company, and then the new employee. To improve the situation, you can talk to the new employee from the perspective of what actions you would like him to take in the future. The idea behind Feedforward is that by focusing on the desired goals, things can progress much more smoothly.

# 5.

## Increasing the level of abstraction for self-absorbed individuals

### Reflecting on the relationship between oneself and others

The level of abstraction, whether high or low, can be influenced by personal experiences and education.

When we talk about "increasing abstraction," the tendency for some individuals is to resist. This can be because the term itself may be unfamiliar to them. However, raising the level of abstraction can help resolve problems more effectively. Encourage them by saying, "Let's try an exercise that will give you the experience of raising your level of abstraction."

Let's start with an introduction to abstract thinking. Imagine there's a can of coffee in front of you.

Person A: What is this?

Person B: It's a can of coffee.

Person A: If we describe it in a broader sense, it's coffee, right? That's increasing the level of abstraction. Now, let's try increasing the level of abstraction a bit further.

Person B: Beverage?

Person A: Exactly. If we raise the level of abstraction a bit more?

Person B: Liquid?

Person A: Yes, exactly. That's how we increase the level of abstraction.

The term *level of abstraction* may seem complex at first, but as demonstrated by this example of a simple exchange, anyone can quickly grasp its meaning. In many cases, people become overwhelmed by focusing solely on their own concerns and troubles. That's why it's important to shift their focus to the relationship between themselves and others. For example, you can say things like, "Let's consider ourselves and the team," or "Let's think about ourselves and the department."

When you have a subordinate who is troubled by his mistake at work, you can ask questions like:

- How does it appear from the team's perspective?
- How does it appear from the department's perspective?
- How does it appear from the company's perspective?

- If we look at it from an industry perspective, how does it appear?

By asking these questions, the level of abstraction naturally increases without explicitly using the term *level of abstraction*. You can explain the concept of level of abstraction later if necessary. Alternatively, you can also approach it from the perspective of the section manager or department manager. During a conversation between a manager and a subordinate, you can ask questions like, "What would you think if you were in my position?" or "How would you approach this if you were in my shoes?" These questions can also increase the level of abstraction.

## When given instructions, they freeze up

In communicating with the millennial generation, it is important to use questioning techniques. If you simply give an instruction such as "Do it this way," it can lead to a mental block. When a young employee from this generation is facing challenges at work, even if a supervisor suggests trying a certain approach, they may not take action readily. However, if you ask them, "What do you think would be the best approach?" the chances are that they will be able to think for themselves and act accordingly.

Specifically with this generation, they won't take action unless they understand their objectives. Moreover, having been raised with praise and approval, they wear a suit of pride. They find it difficult to admit their limitations or a lack of understanding, and they are hesitant to ask questions. They tend to retreat into their own shells. If they are kept in a situation where they don't understand and are expected to continue, they may experience health issues or quickly change jobs.

It is often the case that before gaining experience and developing the foundational skills necessary to perform work, it can be challenging for these individuals to open their mind and make progress. However, when you ask them how they perceive the current situation and what they think should be done, they express their opinions well. Surprisingly, even those who previously struggled to take action and were troubled do come up with excellent ideas that surpass one's imagination.

It is true that everyone has various assumptions and biases in their minds. This can be compared to a state of being brainwashed. To address this, it is necessary to understand and unravel each individuals' assumptions. Increasing the level of abstraction is key to removing these assumptions. While it is up to individuals themselves to let go of their previous programming, skillfully providing feedforward can help anyone, including the millennial generation, to remove assumptions previously made.

There are many situations where it is quicker to simply provide the answer. Let's think about a case where a new employee asks, "What should I do? My computer is acting up." Naturally, it is not productive to respond, "What do you think you should do?" When they want to resolve computer issues, it is best to advise them to contact a computer vendor or the responsible personnel in the company's information systems department. There are many instances where a simple suggestion would suffice, for example, just tell the new employee, "Please contact the person in charge at the Information Systems department for help."

When it comes to wanting them to become proficient in their tasks, it is important to provide thorough feedforward and offer guidance. If it is something that others should support them, it is appropriate to simply tell them how to get help and solve their problems.

## Setting goals and gradually increasing the level of abstraction

By setting goals and gradually increasing the level of abstraction, assumptions and biases gradually fade away. Within the neural networks of our brains, there is a flow of electrical signals. When we consistently use the same circuits, those specific areas get strengthened, and our assumptions become stronger. However, by setting goals, these assumptions can gradually diminish. With new thought patterns being aligned with the goals, new assumptions become necessary, and the old patterns are no longer used.

In the case of the millennial generation, many individuals seem to have the goal of seeking approval. They desire recognition from those around them but may be reluctant to experience any difficult challenges themselves. They may not have a strong desire for career advancement and therefore, may prefer to continue living their lives without facing difficulties. The justification may be that they have managed to get by comfortably thus far.

When approaching the entire millennial generation, it is important to help them understand that seeking approval and wanting to be praised is something specific to their generation. It is essential to guide them toward a stage of understanding that individuals from other generations may not share the same mindset.

To achieve this, it becomes necessary to shake up their perception of what they consider to be normal. Even if they are living in abundance in Japan, exposing them to images of hunger in Africa, for example, can make them realize that such a world exists, momentarily shifting their awareness in that direction.

They need to grasp the fact that a world where being praised is considered normal is not actually the norm, and that there is a reality where receiving praise is not guaranteed. This is a reality that they may find hard to imagine, no matter how much they try to contemplate it on their own.

When the person is ready to listen, it is important to convey the following message clearly and appropriately. You should say, "You always seem to want to be praised, but that's not how it works." Or you can say "Please note that this is not my personal opinion but know that the world doesn't operate in that way."

By expressing it directly like this, they will likely come to realize it. At the very least, it serves as the first step toward awareness. When in a state of looking toward the future through feedforward, even straightforward communication becomes more effective and easier to comprehend.

# 6.

## What you envision in your mind is projected onto others

---

### Choose a place where you can feel a high level of abstraction

When conducting feedforward sessions with clients, I choose locations that offer a clear view of distant scenery. For example, I might choose a lounge on a high floor of a hotel with glass windows overlooking the outside. We sit in a way that allows both of us to face the same direction and enjoy the view of this distant scenery. As we begin the session, we start a conversation with comments like, "It's beautiful weather today, isn't it?"

Usually, in a corporate setting, feedforward is often conducted in a meeting room. In such cases, I personally visualize distant scenery in my mind while progressing with the session. This is because what I imagine in my mind tends to be projected onto the other person's brain. This is actually, one of the discoveries in cognitive science. What I experience with a sense of reality seems to be similarly felt by those who are in close proximity and sharing the same space.

For example, let's say you heard from an acquaintance, "I went to watch a sumo match the other day, and in the final bout, the Yokozuna champion lost, and the seat cushions went flying, causing a commotion." When hearing this, a visualization of seat cushions flying might arise in your mind. Although it may not be an exact replica of your acquaintance's mental image, your brain utilizes prior knowledge to construct the imagery. While not an identical image, what exists in the speaker's mind can be projected into the listener's mind.

Therefore, even if the session takes place in a conference room, if the forwarder maintains a high vantage point in their imagery, looking into the distance, it creates an atmosphere where the receiver also feels as if they are viewing scenery from a higher place, allowing them to focus on their future with a higher level of abstraction. The forwarder will wait, remaining relaxed, maintaining a high-level perspective, with sole consideration for the receiver and trusting that the receiver will shift their consciousness toward their own future.

As mentioned earlier, a crucial aspect attributed to the success of feedforward is *the power of waiting*. This is the essential secret of feedforward. The forwarder believes in the receiver's ability to focus on their own future and patiently waits for the receiver to spontaneously express their thoughts about the future.

The source of this *power of waiting* for the forwarder lies in *the power to believe in themselves*. It should be the firm conviction of the forwarder to state "I can trust and wait for the receiver" and "I am a contributing presence to the receiver's happiness." That is what serves as the secret recipe.

# 7.

# Raising the level of abstraction to solve family issues

## Anyone can be the forwarder in the family

So far, we have looked at feedforward in a business context, but it can be applied to any situation. Feedforward is utilized by directing our focus toward the future and taking action in that direction. The approach remains the same as discussed earlier. The methods can be applied in the same way we have talked about in the other various scenarios.

Let's explore feedforward in a family context. There is a husband who works long hours and often comes home late. His wife also works and takes care of their two children. It can be described as a situation where the wife is handling parenting responsibilities alone, known as *one-parent childcare*. The wife is dissatisfied with her husband's excessive workload and constantly gives him feedback. She suggests that he consider whether it's worth continuing in a stressful job at such a demanding company. She also vents her frustrations to her friends, expressing concerns about her husband's excessive work hours.

The husband is aware of his wife's dissatisfaction but feels helpless with feelings of being overwhelmed with his immediate career demands and doesn't know what to do. Ideally, it would be beneficial for them to seek a third party who can act as a forwarder. This person would provide Feedforward to both of them as receivers. Since terms like *one-parent childcare* and *excessive workload* indicate a relatively low level of abstraction, seeking the assistance of a third party can expedite their progress toward a solution. Alternatively, it can also be possible for either one of them to act as a forwarder and provide Feedforward to the other.

When conducting Feedforward to a couple, it can be helpful to create and share a balance wheel perspective to ensure smooth communication. The *Balance Wheel* is a circular diagram used to visualize multiple goals in various aspects of life. (The *Balance Wheel* will be discussed in detail in Chapter 5.) By sharing their individual goals on the balance wheel, the couple can collectively reflect on their shared future and ask, "What do we want for ourselves?"

In the above case, after feedforwarding to each other, discussing topics that would make them happy as a couple, they made the decision for the wife to quit her job and work as a freelancer. The husband moved to a position where he no longer had to work on-site. After these two adjustments, the wife sees that the husband is doing his best to become involved. If the husband had responded to the wife's feedback with opposition, it could have led to a breakdown in their marriage. However, because both individuals were able to think with a higher level of abstraction, they were able to build a new dynamic to strengthen their relationship.

## Increase the other person's level of abstraction

This is another story of a couple. The husband works for an IT-related company and the wife is a stay-at-home mom who is taking care of their child who attends kindergarten. The wife, feeling the exhaustion of childcare, occasionally vents her frustrations to her husband, usually about once a month.

This is another situation where Feedforward can be effective. First, the husband calmly listens to his wife's words, although he may have felt the urge to say, "But look at all the things I'm doing too, can't you see?" In fact, he occasionally helps with kindergarten drop-offs and takes time off work to participate in school events. However, realizing that engaging in a feedback battle would only make things worse, he remains silent and listens to her as she vents.

The key is to respond with an attitude of understanding, saying things like, "I see. It must be tough. You feel that way, don't you?" It's important to listen from the perspective of the other person, focusing on their concerns rather than shifting the focus back to oneself. While the wife may express dissatisfaction with the husband along the way, it's essential to avoid feeling attacked and instead calmly acknowledge, "So that's how you feel."

While listening, the husband also assesses the level of his wife's abstract thinking. One day, the wife expresses her exhaustion, saying "I am so tired of our child not listening to me." She explains that their child has been playing at the park, in the cold, for a long time and she worries that she will catch a cold while trying to keep up with him.

The husband asks, "Why do you end up going with our son, even though it's cold?" The wife responds, "Our child wants to play. He has started exploring various activities this year, and I feel bad for him. If I take him home, he will be upset. That's why I'm accompanying him." At this stage, the conversation shifts from the wife's condition to the relationship between the wife and their son, indicating an increase in abstract thinking.

At that point, the wife asks, "What do we want as a family?" It raises their abstract thinking level even further. Both of them have dreams of sending their child to an international school and that they in turn would start living overseas as a family. Then the conversation shifts to, "What do we need to do to make that happen?" Then, the wife says, "I want to start studying English."

The key point here is that they raised the level of abstraction. If they engage this conversation with feedback and respond with statements at the same level of abstraction, it may not lead to a resolution. For example, if the wife says, "I'm exhausted because our child doesn't listen and plays in the park in the cold," responding with, "What? Are you worried that our boy would catch a cold. I also go to work even when I have a cold." This kind of interaction won't resolve the issue. This is because they are speaking at the same level of abstraction.

# 8.

## A Feedforward meeting conducted in a format of one-to-many

### Anytime, anywhere

Feedforward can indeed be conducted in various settings, including everyday conversations. For instance, let's say you're attempting to provide feedforward to four individuals. As the forwarder, you would assess the level of abstraction for each individual (receiver) and rephrase your message in a way that resonates with each person.

Feedforward progresses through two types of prompts from the forwarder: questions and the subsequent words after the receiver's response. The subsequent words need to be tailored to the receiver's level of abstraction.

As mentioned earlier, it is important to understand the abstraction level of the other person. Further it is important to encourage them to increase their level of abstraction by just one step. If you jump ahead and discuss topics that are two or three levels above, it may not resonate with them. This also applies when a supervisor is giving advice to a subordinate. For example, when a department head shares advice based on their own experiences with a new employee in their twenties, the advice may not immediately click with the newbie.

There was a case where a new employee in their twenties was assigned to be the person in charge of attracting new attendees to an event. Every day, this young man was monitoring the number of event registrations, and he felt frustrated by the slow progress. As the event day was approaching, he realized that they were still far short from reaching the targeted number of attendees, and he began worrying about the situation. This newbie finally decided to seek advice from his supervisor and senior colleagues during their next event preparation meeting.

During the meeting, the supervisor made a statement, saying, "It's important not to focus solely on immediate numbers (registration count), but to think about the overall success of the event. Particularly in terms of enhancing participant satisfaction. Let's overcome the challenge of low attendance by adding a measure for how attractive the program is perceived to be by the attendee." Upon hearing this, the newbie felt that a burden was lifted off his shoulders. This is because he interpreted the supervisor's words as permission to give up on attracting more attendees.

The event day arrived, and the attendance rate was below 50% of the target. It turned out to be a very disappointing day. The event ended up operating at a loss, dealing a significant revenue blow to the company.

What the supervisor intended to convey were these two points:

1. It is essential to ensure effective audience recruitment as a fundamental prerequisite, while also striving to create an event that increases participant satisfaction.
2. Even at this stage, it is important to brainstorm and promote appealing programs that contribute to attracting attendees, aiming to turn the situation around.

It was obviously the responsibility of the supervisor for the situation. It was challenging for the new employee to comprehend. When someone is presented with a conversation that involves two or three levels above their understanding, it becomes difficult for them to grasp it.

In this case, if the supervisor had said something like, "Let's add attractive ideas that would make participants happy. We would promote those ideas effectively in the hopes that we could turn around the rate of registrations," the new employee might have come up with an effective idea. This incident served as a valuable lesson for the supervisor.

In one-on-one situations, it is sufficient to tailor the conversation to the recipient's level of abstraction. However, when there are multiple recipients, there is a possibility that everyone has a different level of abstraction. In this case, the supervisor failed because he was not addressing the new employee directly but rather speaking to the senior members of the group who shared a higher level of abstraction than this new employee.

**CHAPTER 5**

# Clarifying the Receiver's Goal

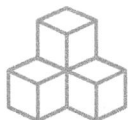

## 1.

### Set a goal beyond the status quo

#### What is a *great* goal?

The forwarder assists the receiver in setting their goals. Focusing on the future, the forwarder asks the receiver, "What do you really want to do?" and "What is the number one thing you want to do?" Asking these questions will enhance the receiver's ability to see their future. Further to this they will gradually be able to see their goals with greater clarity.

Let's see what goals we can set here.

In the Gold Vision Method, a system in which I classify a desirable goal as a *good goal*, and I explain that a good goal must meet three requirements: *Greatness, Wanting to, and Many.*

- Is the goal outside the status quo? (Greatness)
- Is the goal what the receiver truly wants? (Wanting to)
- Do they have many goals instead of just one? (Many)

The first step is to set goals *outside* the status quo. Here is one reason why this is important. When goals are set within the scope of the status quo, the brain can only exercise its ability to maintain the status quo. Humans possess an innate mechanism known as *homeostasis*, a fundamental function that enables the body to maintain its physical and mental conditions within a certain range. This intrinsic ability is exemplified in instances where the body, in its attempt to keep a constant body temperature, releases heat by sweating during hot conditions, and the inverse also applies where the body generates heat through shivering during cold conditions.

The brain also seeks to maintain *the status quo*. If doing nothing to change their situation, one never deviates from this familiar status quo. We refer to this familiar place as the *Comfort Zone*. The Comfort Zone not only encompasses the physical location but also the cognitive space we experience within our mind. However, it's important to note that the Comfort Zone does not always equate to a comfortable environment. For instance, even if one cannot earn as much as they desire, they can become accustomed to that situation and adopt it as their Comfort Zone.

It is of particular importance to set goals outside of the status quo in order to fully exercise the power of the brain. What precisely does *outside the status quo* refer to? Here are a couple of key examples.

Google's vision, as a company that maintains a world-class brand value, is to create a world where access to information from around the globe is made possible with just a single click. This vision may seem commonplace today, but how many individuals could envision such a world before the existence of Google? By setting this ambitious goal, the founders and employees of the company made full use of their intellectual abilities. Their goal has largely come to fruition.

When Softbank President Masayoshi Son launched his company, he stood on a box for packing oranges and declared, "We will build a trillion-yen company over the next few decades." At the time, SoftBank was still a small company and all the part-timers and employees who had to hear his grandiose vision rolled their eyes. The result was predictable as some even left the company having lost trust in the leadership. However, as you know, SoftBank has since developed into a large organization, just as Mr. Son declared.

## Near goals are more difficult to achieve

One of the responsibilities of the forwarder in a feedforward session is to expand the goal for the receiver. When the receiver discusses the goal they have in mind, the forwarder then poses the question, "Would you like to make it even bigger?"

I suppose it's an old habit, but when we set goals in a normal manner, they often end up being just a slight improvement from the status quo. For instance, we may set a goal like *a 5% increase from the previous year*. However, goals that only slightly surpass the status quo are perceived by the brain as being *part of the status quo* and therefore do not engage your brains' performance abilities. From the brain's point of view, *a 5% increase* is the same as *doing next to nothing*.

With a goal of this level, the brain decides that everything is fine as it is, and the energy in not generated to transform this stable state. Therefore, no additional activity is performed to realize the goal. This makes it unlikely that the goal will actually be realized.

This may sound a bit extreme but if you can currently run only 1 mile were to set a goal of 5% increase, being able to run 1.05 miles in three months, undoubtedly, you would not do anything special. But what if you set the goal of completing a full marathon of 26.2 miles in three months?

If you don't practice, you will never achieve this goal. It is most likely you will naturally begin to practice.

Similarly, when a person with an annual income of $50,000 aims for $80,000 per year or a person with a TOEIC[3] score of 400 aims for a score of 600 on the TOEIC, no additional energy is generated because these goals are an extension of the status quo for the brain.

To get the brain to produce additional energy, the goal must be set high.

For example, if a person with an annual income of $50,000 sets a goal of $500,000 per year or a person with a TOEIC score of 400 points sets a goal of 950 points on the TOEIC (which at first glance may seem impossible) the brain will begin to think outside the status quo. This will generate a giant leap in thinking. This will produce ideas and results that are in an entirely different dimension than that of the status quo.

When we focus on the mechanism of cognition, by setting goals outside of the status quo, the RAS (Reticular Activating System) starts working in the world of those goals. The RAS starts to selectively bring relevant information into consciousness based on its importance. As a result, only the information necessary for achieving the goals will be raised into consciousness. Information unrelated to the goals will remain hidden behind the scotoma (blind spot) and will not come into your consciousness. This allows us to concentrate

---

3 "TOEIC: The Test of English for International Communication is an international standardized test of English language proficiency for non-native speakers, with the highest possible score 990."

and advance efficiently toward the achievement of our set goals. I would like to reiterate that the major energy generated by a high-level goal is not just because the spirit is willing; it essentially occurs as an inevitable result of the physical mechanism of the brain and cognitive functions.

The feedforward process provides some insights for creating great goals. For example, we can offer the question: "Can you increase it more?" This is the simplest way to pose the question of adding more. You can increase the targeted income or asset amount by one or two digits. Increasing the number of your friends is another example of increasing the number.

Another question would be, "Can you extend the duration?" This is a question that should be asked to dramatically increase a duration of time required to achieve goals. For example, your life expectancy, or the length of time you can work until retirement.

Alternatively, you can ask, "Do you know how to achieve that goal?" A great way to determine if a goal is within or outside of your status quo is as follows. If we know how to achieve a goal, then we know that the goal is *within the status quo*. If we are unsure of how to achieve the goal, then it is likely to be *outside the status quo*.

### Raise the level of abstraction of the goal

You can make it a *great* goal by increasing the *level of abstraction*, which we discussed in Chapter 4.

For example, becoming the president of your company

is actually a goal that is an extension of the status quo. Becoming a president itself is a challenging endeavor, but whether or not you can become a president, given that they are already an employee, is a matter of probability. Subconsciously, you brain believes it is an extension of the current situation.

Therefore, by greatly increasing the level of abstraction of the goal from *wanting to become a president* to *engaging in work that transforms the industry*, you can turn this goal into a great goal.

As the level of abstraction increases for your goal, the number of people you are influencing also increases. If the initial goal is *to obtain qualifications and improve my level of work*, by changing it *to become a master in my field and create my own higher qualification system,* the number of people influenced by the second goal will significantly increase as compared to the first.

Forwarders, in essence, spontaneously expand on their own thoughts during the feedforward session, thinking, "Wouldn't it be great if it turned out like this?" while listening to the receiver's story. They immerse themselves in the receiver's perspective and freely feedforward and help to expand the story of the receivers' future. By doing so, the receiver's level of abstraction also increases, and the goals become grandiose and impressive. As the receivers themselves experience this process, they are able to envision a new world for which they mostly feel gratitude.

# 2.

## Is the goal something you desire to do?

---

### Doing what you want generates power.

Making the goal bigger is important, but it's essential to ensure that it aligns with what the receiver truly wants. When we set a bigger goal without considering our genuine desires, we might end up realizing it's not something we really wanted.

When your heart is truly in what you aspire to do, energy will naturally surge within you. As previously mentioned, this is the second element of a good goal: *Wanting to*. Have you encountered a moment when you were so absorbed in what you were passionate about that you felt fine without sleeping or eating? Once you're able to set a goal based on what you want to do, you will enter this kind of state.

To gain a deeper understanding of *wanting to*, let's consider the following scenario. Consider the goal of becoming president. I mentioned that this goal is not very abstract, but it also lacks power in terms of wanting to do it. Without a clear vision of what you want to accomplish as a president, the brain does not function effectively.

Furthermore, unless the wanting-to is *what you really want to do from the bottom of your heart*, the brain will not follow through. No matter how cool you say it, it must be sincere. The brain sees through the pretense.

By the way, upon hearing the receiver's goal you may sometimes wonder, "Really? Is that what you *really* want?"

When a receiver tells you about a somewhat unexpected goal, you can confirm by asking, "Oh, I see. So that's what you want to do?" If a receiver is trying to set a *great* goal such as "I want to go on a trip to Mars," you can ask, "I see. So, you really want to go there?" The receiver may respond, "Hmmm, well, when I think about it, maybe it's not that appealing after all." This means that the person tried to set a *big* goal as suggested, but it was not something he/she genuinely wanted to any degree.

Someone who previously expressed a desire to become number one in their industry, ended up reevaluating their ambition and concluded that it's not necessarily so. Similarly, a person who once wished for a private jet may say, "Upon further consideration, I don't think it's necessary." The correction of such realizations is left entirely to the receiver.

Even if you, as the forwarder, are taken aback during a session you should accept whatever the receiver says and simply reply with "Oh, I see." Then you help the receiver boost the sense of reality when the goal has been achieved. Through this process of imagining the goal achievement and feeling the sense of reality, the receiver may realize that the goal they initially set will not really make them happy. If this is the case the receiver will change his/her goal to something else.

## The Goal Comes First, Then We Perceive

The goal-achieving mechanism based on cognitive science

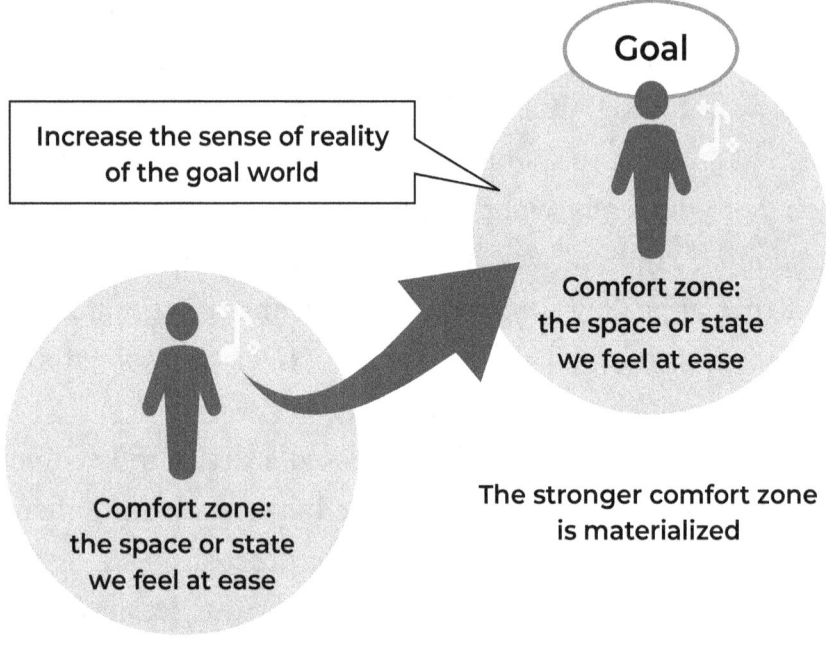

---

# 3.

## Are there many goals?

---

### The synergy of many goals

We all want to be happy. Happiness has many elements.

For businesspeople work may occupy a large percentage of their time but everyone has a part outside of work, call it a non-work aspect. At the office, you may be a section manager, at home you may be a father, mother, husband, or wife. From a parent's perspective you are a child, if you attend a school, you are a student, and from a neighbor's perspective you are a neighbor.

There are people who stick to one thing and pursue it to its fullest and I think that is a wonderful way to live. However, life is made up of many different elements, including work, family, friends, hobbies, and social responsibility, and even if you fully achieve only one of those elements, you may not be so happy if the rest are left unfulfilled.

It seems common for businesspeople who have worked from early in the morning until late at night to lose sight of their goals and become foggy when they retire. In some severe cases, relationships with family members who have been neglected for years may break down, leading to a solitary life in old age.

To become happier, you need to cover many aspects of your life, and you need to establish as many goals as possible. I recommend listing at least eight areas that are important to you and setting a goal for each of them.

## Setting Goals with a Balance Wheel

A diagram called the *Balance Wheel* will help organize this process. Things that are important to your life may include the following:

| | |
|---|---|
| Occupation goals | Family goals |
| Hobbies goals | Friends goals |
| Health goals | Finance goals |
| Retirement Goals | Social contribution goals |

These are some of the categories we can think about. The name *Balance Wheel* is filled with my belief that happiness is achieved when happiness lies in setting multiple goals and achieving them in a balanced manner. Feeling happy becomes challenging if just one of your eight goals is accomplished, and the rest remain unfulfilled.

For example, consider the following scenario:

- I am contributing to society, but I struggle financially to make ends meet every day.
- I have achieved an annual income of $1 million, but my family relationships are terrible.

Particularly in Japan, work and finance tend to receive most of the emphasis. This tends to impede the achievement of other goals. It is all too common to hear how people become so absorbed in their work. So much that they fail to take care of their families. In such cases, what I would like you to be conscious of is the level of abstraction that is one step higher than each individual goal.

In other words, we would like to remind you of the perspective that individual goals exist solely for happiness. This also means that each goal is equally important, and the lack of any one of them will reduce the level of happiness.

# Balance Wheel
Having multiple goals is desirable for everyone
Set a high goal for each category

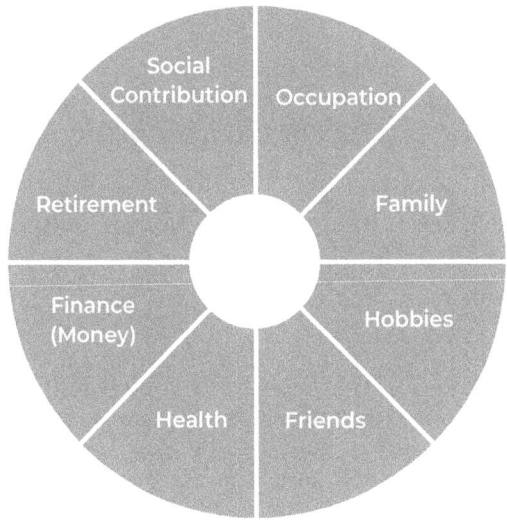

## Occupation

- Continuously developing products (services) that are always in demand by our customers.
- Overwhelmingly stable work performance, earning the trust of those around me.
- Supporting my supervisor by acting as a coordinator for the members around me.
- Delving into my own area of expertise and being unique in my field.
- Discovering a career that I genuinely want to pursue and enjoy working in every day.

## Family

- The children are growing up freely and confidently, being true to themselves.
- My spouse is living a healthy and happy life.
- My parents are enjoying their retirement free from worries.
- My family is full of smiles.

## Hobbies

- Cycling: I take two bicycle trips each year, one in the spring and one in the fall.
- Golf: I play golf about twice a month, my score is improving, and I enjoy it.
- Temple visits: Whenever I make a trip, I visit temples in town and appreciate the diverse experiences each one provides.
- Travel: Several times a year, I visit the places I want to go without any time restrictions.
- Cooking: I enjoy cooking what I am good at and savoring it with the people I love.
- Fashion: I enjoy wearing my favorite outfits every day, embracing the joy of fashion.

## Friend

- I enjoy spending time with friends of all ages both at home and abroad.
- I plan fun events with my friends and invite new people to these gatherings, expanding my circle of friends even further.
- I get together with my friends from school once a year to strengthen our friendship.
- I make many friends in the community by volunteering for the local festival.

## Health

- I eat a healthy diet every day.
- I am getting the sleep I need to stay energized every day.
- I try to find time to relax and clear my mind.

## Finance

- I earn XXX a year in a job I truly enjoy.
- I have been building assets methodically, and at some point in the future, I will have YYY assets.

**Retirement**
- I am living a happy retirement with good health, family, friends, money, etc.

**Social responsibilities**
- I make monthly donations of ZZZ to Organization ABC.
- I regularly engage in community service activities that require me to physically exert myself.

---

## Have a balance wheel drawn up before the session

Ideally, it is easier to carry on the conversation if you have your subordinate draw up a balance wheel before the session. Thanks to this balance wheel exercise, individuals who have solely focused on their work goals will start discussing their goals in other aspects of life.

Using the balance wheel in workplace-feedforward meetings allows you to have conversations with your subordinates about non-work-related matters as well. (However, it's not mandatory to disclose goals if some individuals prefer not to.)

For example, suppose that during a feedforward meeting between a supervisor and a subordinate, the balance wheel reveals that the subordinate is having trouble at home or with friends. In this sort of situation, the conversation may proceed like this:

Supervisor: I don't think I can help you with that, but things get easier when work is going well.

Subordinate: Yes, that's true.

Supervisor: All right, then let's get right down to talking about our work today.

One might doubt whether work and hobbies can be discussed together. Hobbies and work both share similarities in how they are approached. Both involve setting goals, making plans, and taking action to achieve them.

The difference is encompassed in the answer to the question, "whom do you do it for?" A hobby pleases only yourself. However, work is performed to satisfy someone else, like a customer, rather than solely for personal gratification. Interestingly, due to their shared structure, putting effort into your hobby can surprisingly enhance your job performance as well.

You can make a goal more powerful by writing it down and writing it down in a certain way. For example, writing a goal down using the verb tense and wording it in a way as if the goal has already been achieved. These are a few examples showing the *from* to the *to* version.

- I want to have the financial resources to do all the things my family wants to do. ➡ I have the financial resources to do all the things my family wants to do.
- I want to get along with my husband. ➡ I get along well with my husband.
- I want to meet a nice person. ➡ I am happy that I have met a nice person.

- My friends are achieving success. ➡ In their respective fields, my friends are flourishing and achieving remarkable success.

As in the examples above, express the goals to show that they have been achieved and are ongoing. This is because the brain cannot distinguish between what has happened and what is perceived and not yet happened. By describing a goal as if it has already happened, the brain perceives the goal as having already been achieved. Although the brain feels unsettled with the fact that the goal has not happened. This contradiction is what produces the energy to make it happen, pushing us toward the achievement of the goal.

## Understanding that the goals of others are different from our own

This is a story about a TV station director. She often hears the president talk about the situation in the context of "Today's TV industry is…". The president hopes that his employees elevate their *level of abstraction* and think about what is beneficial, not only for the company but for the entire industry. However, she thinks that if she can deliver good content, any medium will do. She does not hold strong feelings about the future of the industry.

This is because there is a gap between the president's goal and the director's goal as their goals are different. It would be beneficial for the president to understand the director's goals for the purpose of working with her toward finding a shared vision for the future. However, if the president mistakenly assumes that the director has the same goal as the president, conflicts may arise.

There is no reason for a problem to exist, especially when this director is creating excellent content that will be positive for the TV industry. However, if the president asks the director to think on the abstract level of the industry as a whole, the director may shy from taking on that much responsibility and that becomes an unnecessary burden. Surprisingly, this kind of misunderstanding can be one of the causes as to why employees quit from their positions.

In such cases, it is important to understand that each person has their own goals. By providing feedforward to one another, you can elevate the relationship to a new level of collaboration.

# 4.

## Always affirm the receiver's goals

### Imagine what it will be like when the goal is achieved

It is also effective to imagine specifically what it will be like when a goal is achieved. For example, consider asking the following questions to someone who has set the goals of getting married while continuing with their job and living abroad:

> "One year from today, when you wake up in the morning, all of your wishes have come true. What do you

think this would look like for you? When you wake up in the morning and see your face in the mirror. How would your face look like in that mirror?"

"I think I will have a big smile on my face."

"What will you do after that?"

"I will go to work and greet everyone with a smile on my face."

Even if there are people who believe that their wishes will never come true, feedforward can dramatically increase the possibility of their wishes being fulfilled. The important thing for the forwarder is to affirm the receiver's goal.

In the world, even if you set good goals, there may be times when people around you deny or ridicule your aspirations, saying "It's impossible," or questioning "Why you keep talking about it?" In such situations, your spirit may diminish. Parental influence will also play a major role in this.

When a parent accurately understands a child's wish and expresses support by saying, "That will be great if you can make it happen," the child develops a sense of validation toward their own desires. However, at times, parents may discourage their children's goals by stating, "Don't dwell on that, focus on what's right in front of you."

For example, when a child expresses a wish to become a famous person, and they are repeatedly told, "That's for special people, instead of saying such things, focus on studying for your exams." They will gradually lose the ability to affirm their aspiration. In contrast, Forwarders will never become *dream killers*, no matter what happens.

Forwarders always respect the receiver's goals. They do not interfere with the overall quality of their goals, nor do they raise any particular concerns. If it is something the person wants to pursue, they offer their full support.

However, a forwarder can decide in advance that they will not support a particular person. For example, I have decided that I will not support anyone who is trying to disrupt the peace. This is because if I feedforward to terrorists, they will only grow in power.

## Feedforward clarifies targets

Forwarders can also help clarify goals and targets (short-term objectives) for the receivers.

Let's consider the case of a general manager who is concerned about the frequent conflicts within the company. This manager's goal is to "cultivate improved relationships in each department within one year," so the forwarder helps the manager increase their sense of reality assuming their target has been achieved.

"What would make you happy?"

"I want all the internal strife to end."

"When that happens, what would it be like?"

"Hopefully we can all get together for a year-end party."

"You mean that you can't all get together now, right?"

"That's right. We plan, but less than half of them show up."

"That's too bad. Where would the best place be to have a year-end party?"

"Perhaps a Japanese tavern (izakaya)."

"I see. An izakaya?"

"Well, let me think. Currently, the entire company is working on a project. When it successfully finishes up, it would be nice if we could be so bold that we rent out a lounge in a luxury hotel for the party."

"What kind of food dishes are lined up in front of you?"

"Maybe Italian."

"Who do you see attending the party?"

"All of the employees are attending."

"How's everyone doing at the party?"

"They all seem to be having fun and enjoying their wine."

"What kind of outfit are you wearing?"

"I am wearing a sharper suit than I am right now."

"What color?"

"Dark blue."

"How do you feel then?"

"We have accomplished the project with all the employees, and we are feeling relieved and fulfilled."

"Are you talking to your subordinates?"

"Yes, I am."

"What are you talking about?"

"I am apologizing for not communicating well when I first became general manager the year before."

"But how are you feeling with your subordinates at the moment?"

"I am feeling comfortable enough with them to laugh and talk about it."

This is the *visualized* future state. You experience a specific image in your mind of how you want to be and the state you want to achieve. At that moment, your brain perceives the goal and target as having already been accomplished. At this point, your brain generates strong energy toward achieving that goal and target.

# 5.

## Comfort zones shift when goals are set

---

### Two comfort zones

When you set a big goal that resides well beyond the status quo, your sense of the reality of this *goal world* increases to a high-enough level in which two comfort zones appear.

They are:

1. The status quo comfort zone that you are now accustomed to, and
2. The comfort zone in the goal world, where you have set a goal and projected yourself into it.

However, this is only hypothetical. You cannot have two co-existing comfort zones because the human brain can only maintain one comfort zone at a time. Even if you use feedforward to gain some sense of reality of a goal world that exists at a higher level, that alone may bring you back to your current comfort zone where you feel a stronger sense of reality.

This is the reason why the efforts we undertake for self-improvement, such as acquiring qualifications, learning a language, dieting, jogging, and more, often fail to be sustained over time. While we may initially feel the reality of the comfort zone in being slim by dieting, our subconscious mind may intervene with thoughts like, "If it's this difficult, it's fine to stay a bit overweight," or "I would find more happiness indulging in delicious food." Consequently, we tend to remain within the status quo comfort zone.

## Experiencing the imagined comfort zone with a sense of reality

In feedforward, we ask the receivers for an image of their goal. For instance, if there is a new employee who expresses a desire to become a president of a company in the future, you would ask questions like,

- Do you want to become a president?
- What kind of work would you be doing as a president?
- What changes would you like to make as a president? And so on.

(Of course, as mentioned earlier, *becoming president* is not a good goal, but we respect the receiver's wishes and proceed with feedforward using these questions first.)

Then, the receiver's sense of reality in the goal world increases. When their sense of reality is raised high enough, they start to think: "Something is not right. Why am I not the president yet?" They start feeling uneasy subconsciously and start working very hard toward their dream goal. The brain becomes activated, striving to bridge the gap between its desired destination and its current position.

Nevertheless, a new employee does not suddenly become the company president. This means that the receiver has begun to move from the status quo of being a new employee toward the place they aim for – being the president – and translate this to doing their current job well. By doing so, they will become a section chief earlier than their peers, then a general manager, and quickly ascend the ladder one step at a time. In the process, they often find a much better goal than becoming president.

## Shake up your comfort zone

Facilitating the receiver's exposure to an experience outside the comfort zone is an effective method for easing the transition and enabling them to shift their comfort zone. Once you have an experience outside of your comfort zone, you feel "I see, this is how it is."

In our daily lives, we often remain within the familiar boundaries of our comfort zone without realizing it. Therefore, my suggestion is for you to deliberately try something that might seem to be beyond your normal limits or try something that you would never do under normal circumstances.

Everyone has his/her own way of taking a bold step: eating dinner at a luxury hotel, attending an expensive seminar and talking with the participants, going on a solo trip abroad, taking a long bike ride, entering a full marathon, etc. Just be sure to choose something you would like to do.

When we maintain a repetitive routine day after day, our brain's usage becomes fixed and predictable. However, by trying something beyond our limits, we activate circuits that are typically dormant or underutilized.

A woman who didn't speak English or French went on a business trip to France. She was accompanied by an interpreter and numerous other travelers, so the language barrier was not much of a problem. However, when she later traveled by herself to Geneva, Switzerland to visit an acquaintance, she became acutely aware that being able to speak English more fluently would have made it a much more enjoyable trip.

She had always wanted to learn a language, but after the experience of being outside of her comfort zone in Geneva, her comfort zone completely shifted. To bridge the gap between where she wanted to go (communicating naturally in English with people from other countries) and her status quo (not being able to communicate as she wanted), she began naturally to learn English.

Another way of shaking up your comfort zone is to meet people. There was a male junior high school student who tended to miss school frequently. He didn't find studying interesting and avoided socializing with his friends by staying home. However, one day he was inspired by a television program featuring a small robot riding a bicycle and walking on a tightrope.

The boy said to his father, "I want to make something like that." His father responded, "Okay, let's go meet the person who made it and ask him how he did it." The boy was surprised, but quietly nodded his head. The father did some research and found the creator of this robot and went with the boy to one of his lectures. After the lecture, the boy asked the creator of the robot many questions. The boy became interested in building robots and began to study at school again.

Once you have decided on the direction you want to go, you make a change in the status quo to trigger a shift in your comfort zone. That means it shakes up the comfort zone. This activity is voluntary on the part of the receiver. The forwarder advises the receiver, "If there is something you've wanted to do but have not done it yet, why not take this opportunity to do it?"

## You can become a dream killer for yourself

One of the major obstacles to achieving your goals is the presence of a *dream killer*. Dream killers are the ones who actively prevent you from achieving your goals. Surprisingly, the biggest dream killer can often be yourself. However, family members and close acquaintances can also become dream killers.

Let's suppose your goal is "I am utilizing my English skills in doing business overseas." The people around you might kill your dream by saying the following:

- You're not even good at English. How could you possibly do that?
- That worries me because it's not safe to live abroad.

Comfort zones exist both at an individual level and within collective contexts. There are various forces that strive to uphold the status quo and resist change. When you try to go out of the status quo on your own, the subconscious minds of those around you may perceive that the comfort zone, which you maintained with them, is breaking up. This occurs because comfort zones are not solely shaped by individuals but are also formed and maintained by groups.

Some dream killers belong to the category of *in-the-first-place*. For example, they may say, "Is there a need in doing business overseas in the first place?" Such skepticism can be disheartening. In fact, some may even question if the goal is even worth achieving. The only way we can deal with dream killers is by assuming that it is their nature to say such things and to just let their skepticism go. Another approach is to keep your goals a secret, preventing you from being discouraged by the dream killer who may say something disheartening to you.

For many people, the biggest dream killer is within themselves saying, "If you have time to study English, you should be focusing on your work." "It is better to do well in Japan than to compete abroad." These are all excuses to stay in your comfort zone. If your faith in yourself wavers, beware of the dream killer within.

# 6.

## As Feedforward proceeds, expect resistance

### Isn't it better to stay the same?

Right around the time when the Feedforward Action (FFA) process is working, and life is beginning to turn around, stagnation may occur. This is an unconscious force that wants to maintain the status quo comfort zone. This is called resistance to change.

This happens both for oneself and for others. The force that suggests "it would be better to remain the same" actively seeks negative information regarding the desired goal while at the same time highlighting positive aspects to maintaining the status quo.

Mrs. C left the company to start her own business and work as a marketing consultant. During the time she was working for the company, she worked in marketing and public relations. Her husband is a lawyer, and they have a good life. However, her own business was not performing well.

When I first met her, she wasn't doing well. As we carried out the feedforward process, she gradually became more positive, until one day she contacted me with this message. "Could we postpone our session scheduled for the day after tomorrow?" "Okay, let's postpone until the X$^{th}$."

However, as the date was approaching, I received a call from her one more time, saying, "I am sorry, but could we please postpone the session again? I'm not feeling well" I thought to myself, "It's starting."

I got a call to reschedule for the third time because she had numbness in her hands and feet, so I replied, "Even if you're not feeling well, please try to make it to the session." But when I met with her, she did not seem sick. This phenomenon is called *comfort zone sickness*.

The brain can fear changes that might occur within us. In a certain timing, the brain starts causing various activities to obstruct us moving forward. In my client's case, her subconscious caused physical discomfort, such as feeling unwell or numbness in her limbs, to prevent her from meeting with me. From her brain's perspective, meeting with me would lead her to move forward. It's all the work of the subconscious mind.

The remedy lies in recognizing that it is the *comfort zone sickness* when such conditions arise. By breaking free from this shell, the future will genuinely start to transform.

Now, Mrs. C can create her own future. She is currently being asked to do work for large companies, and at the same time, she has established another corporation and started a business that only she can do.

## Goals are not achieved forever

I've now discussed goals. During feedforward sessions, receivers may occasionally ask me, "If I set a high goal, is it guaranteed that I will always achieve it?" Unfortunately, goals are not always achieved. Nevertheless, it is an undeniable truth that setting high goals can greatly propel us toward achieving them.

Furthermore, goals are in a constant state of evolution. By definition this occurs as we update and refine our goals as we are on the verge of achieving them. One could argue that a goal is never truly attained because it continually undergoes updates. While we may reach significant milestones along the way, the final goal remains elusive. The ongoing process of updating our goal serves as the driving force that propels us forward.

Certainly, it is perfectly acceptable to celebrate, such as throwing an achievement party when you surpass an initial goal or milestone. However, it is desirable to maintain a mindset that continuously anticipates that there is more to come. Ideally, the celebration should not be solely focused on past achievements but should serve as a pre-celebration of future accomplishments. It becomes a joyous acknowledgment and anticipation of what lies ahead.

CHAPTER 6

# Enhancing Receiver's Efficacy

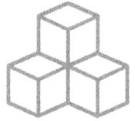

## 1.

**Believe confidently and wholeheartedly,**
*I can do it*

### Why do you think you can do it?

Firmly believing in yourself and your abilities so that you can say, "I can do it." The fact that you can say you can do it is crucial as you move toward the future. When you declare that you *can't do* something, this cancels your ability and motivation. Ultimately, *can do* or *can't do* is a person's subjective judgment.

If you believe you can, you can; if you think you can't, you can't. At this point, the past is of no use to you. Our past achievements may seem valuable, but the true usefulness lies in our abilities themselves that enabled those past accomplishments possible. We can rely on these past abilities, only if they are still present today. For example, if a man could run the 100m in approximately 11-seconds when he was in high school, that would be quite fast. However, if he cannot run at that speed today, it doesn't carry any significance beyond the fact that he was fast in the past. Indeed, every endeavor begins with zero achievements, and regardless of past accomplishments, it is the belief in one's capability that sparks the energy to succeed.

Therefore, when we feedforward, we focus on the positive aspects and potential outcomes. We direct our attention toward the future, confidently affirming that *we can achieve what we desire* or, even better, that *we have already accomplished it.*

Today, it is commonplace for Japanese players to be active in Major League Baseball. This is because they believe that they can play an active role in the Major Leagues. However, as recently as 20 years ago, no one thought that they could.

In 1995, Hideo Nomo, former pitcher for the Kintetsu Buffaloes (now known as the Osaka Kintetsu Buffaloes), bravely embarked on a challenge to play in the Major

Leagues. Despite achieving considerable success in Japan, with 78 victories over five years and earning a salary of 140 million yen ($1.4 million), Nomo made the bold decision to move to the US to pursue his career in the Major Leagues. Initially, the entire Japanese baseball community was against Nomo's decision as there were "no established rules or precedents for such a move." Nevertheless, Nomo didn't give up on his dream, choosing to retire from professional baseball in Japan and venture into the Major Leagues. It is reported that he earned an annual salary of $100,000 in his first year in the Major Leagues.

Since the beginning of the 1995 season, when Nomo took on the role of the rotating pitcher, he achieved remarkable success. With 13 wins and 236 strikeouts, he earned both the Rookie of the Year and Strikeout King titles, solidifying his position as a pioneering Japanese Major Leaguer. During his impressive 14-year career in the Major Leagues, Nomo secured 123 victories.

Nomo's successes undoubtedly shifted the mindset of many Japanese players. The transformation was from a state of doubting their abilities with *I can't do it,* to embracing the confidence with *I can do it*. This transformation played a pivotal role in inspiring the current success of Japanese Major Leaguers.

Hidetoshi Nakata is considered the pioneer among soccer players, with Yasuhiko Okudera being an esteemed predecessor. However, Nakata's influence on today's players is likely more significant. Following the 1998 World Cup in

France, Nakata made a significant move to join Perugia in Italy's Series A. In a last-ditch effort, Nakata terminated his contract with his former club, Bellmare Hiratsuka (at that time), and ventured into an overseas league. This bold move meant that if he faced failure, he couldn't easily return to Japan. Nonetheless, Nakata persevered and played for renowned clubs such as Perugia, AS Roma, Parma, Fiorentina, and others. His success served as a catalyst for the subsequent careers of Shinji Ono, Shunsuke Nakamura, Keisuke Honda, and Shinji Kagawa. They were inspired by Nakata's achievements and followed his path to make a mark in the soccer world.

In the 100-meter track and field race, no Japanese athlete had ever managed to break the 10-second barrier. However, in 2017, Yoshihide Kiryu made history by becoming the first Japanese athlete to break the 10-second mark, clocking in at 9.98 seconds. This remarkable feat has paved the way for more 9-second records in the future. Kiryu's achievement shattered the belief that Japanese athletes couldn't surpass the 10-second barrier.

Observing others succeed influences both our conscious and subconscious minds, fostering the belief that *We can do it too.*

## Efficacy refers to the extent of one's belief that *I can do it*

*Efficacy* is defined as the self-evaluation of one's capabilities to produce desired results. In other words, it represents a level of belief, *I can do it.* I also call this efficacy; *the power to believe in yourself.*

Self-esteem is a concept that is frequently confused with efficacy. Self-esteem is the self-evaluation of one's own worth, which is established based on past achievements and accomplishments, including a self-assessment of the current situation. Self-esteem can be described as the product of the past, while efficacy can be described as the ability to believe in the future.

When efficacy is high, you can progress confidently toward your goals. Efficacy plays an important role in many scenes that contribute to daily life, including work, family, and study. Believing in *I cannot do it* or *I'm no good, anyway* creates limitations that hinder the achievement of results. Conversely, associating oneself with *I can do more* or *I am fully capable* unlocks one's potential and leads to higher achievements.

By holding the belief, "I am a good communicator and I genuinely believe in my ability to build strong relationships with anyone," you unlock the potential to connect with numerous people and thrive in diverse fields. It has been shown that individuals with high efficacy spend more time learning and end up achieving higher grades.

Moreover, individuals with high levels of efficacy are more inclined to take proactive steps toward their goals. They possess the courage to embark on their journey smoothly and take that crucial first step. Even in the face of failures and challenges, they persist in taking action without giving up. The self-efficacy of an *I-can-do-it* attitude results in the desired outcome.

### Efficacy is determined by the future

So, what should we do to increase *efficacy*?

To achieve this, you need to understand both *Conscious-Me* and *Subconscious-Me*. *Conscious-Me* is the source of thoughts and judgments that rise to your consciousness, and it is the aspect of self that can be consciously controlled.

And another particularly important aspect is the *Subconscious-Me*, which resides in the subconscious and therefore operates in a way that is hard to perceive, carrying out thoughts and judgments of oneself that are not conscious. Consciously controlling the *Subconscious-Me*, is nearly impossible.

Feedforward works specifically on the *Subconscious-Me*. The *Conscious-Me* tends to block feedforward because it lives in the present, but the *Subconscious-Me* does not. For example, when you – as a receiver - hear a story with a high level of abstraction from the forwarder, your reaction may be relatively mild like "Oh, I didn't know that," but the *Subconscious-Me* becomes deeply influenced.

For example, when someone tells you, "I took a cabin cruiser out to sea the other day and caught a marlin," and you receive an invitation to join them next time, your conscious response might be, "Well, I'd like to go, but I'm a little nervous." Meanwhile, subconsciously you may start harboring questions like, "What kind of ocean conditions will we be going into?" or "What preparations are needed to catch a marlin?" Before you realize it, your subconscious mind is projecting into the future, and strengthening the reality of the future experience.

Feedforward changes the receiver's *Subconscious-Me.*

# 2.

## Increase efficacy through Feedforward

### Check the receiver's efficacy level

Feedforward is one of the best techniques that can be used to increase efficacy. As you become attuned to the future and work toward it, your efficacy naturally increases. The forwarder needs to be mindful of the receiver's level of abstraction. A helpful approach for the forwarder in achieving this is to observe their self-talk.

Self-talk refers to the words we communicate to ourselves, and the type of self-talk, whether it is *can-do* or *can't-do,* significantly impacts our efficacy. Depending on which of these types are dominant in our mind will give a good indication of how they influence our efficacy.

Improving self-talk naturally leads to an increase in efficacy.

Self-talk is cumulative, and it could have some drawbacks. If you've been repeating the *"can't-do"* type of self-talk since birth, say for 30 years, those words have accumulated in your subconscious mind. It's fair to say that the

*Subconscious-Me* is created by this self-talk. The *Subconscious-Me* is the source of the *bubble-up* self-talk.

Daily self-talk can be improved with conscious effort, but if you have been consistently repeating the *can't do* self-talk throughout your entire life, it can create an overwhelmingly negative *can't-do* state of mind. I will explain self-talk in more detail later.

## A standard of money that lowers the efficacy

Besides *self-talk*, three other factors can significantly influence in lowering the efficacy: *money, time, and other people*. These are further defined as the *standard of money*, the *standard of time*, and the *standard of other people*. When we become entangled in these three limitations, our ability to believe in ourselves is substantially diminished.

If you are obsessed with the *standard of money*, your efficacy will not go up. Feeling overwhelmed when you meet a rich person is a sign that you are preoccupied with the concept of money. You would not feel daunted by meeting someone who weighs more than you. Nor would you feel daunted by meeting someone who can drink more beer than you. You would not feel daunted by meeting someone who collects more of something than you do. However, feeling intimidated by someone wealthy, which wouldn't normally be the case, is evidence of being influenced by the standard of money.

This mindset might lead you to think, "The person with more money is better" or "I can't do something because I don't have money, but they can because they have money," which weakens *the power of believing in yourself*. In a capitalist society, this *standard of money* holds significant influence over and dominates many people. To liberate my clients from the control of the standard of money, I encourage them to tear up a 10,000-yen bill which is equivalent to a 100-dollar bill.

By tearing up the bill, they recognize that a 10,000 yen or 100-dollar bill is just a piece of paper. Even if the meaning of this does not ring true to the conscious mind, it has a great impact on the subconscious. When the subconscious understands that the money you were obsessed with was just paper, the standard of money begins to collapse.

The idea that making a lot of money is better is replaced by the idea that higher goals are more important than higher income, which naturally leads to a more fulfilling life.

## The assumption that time flows from the past

Another thought process that limits efficacy is past-oriented thinking. Setting high goals for the future becomes challenging if you think with a foundation based on past experiences. If you think in terms of your past achievements, a high goal will seem like a pipe dream. As an example, "I am now being treated coldly at the company because the project I lead did not go well at that time." This kind of thinking should be called the curse of causality. It is quite difficult to set a high goal with this mindset. In fact, even if the project went well, you do not know if you would have been treated well or not. There are many factors to consider in human resources matters.

What is important should be the future, not the past, but if you are bound by the *standard of time*, you may think like this:

- I failed before; so, I'll fail again.
- My life is no good because I failed the college entrance exam.
- Growing up with parents who constantly denied me from a very young age has led me to perceive myself negatively.

This negative way of thinking should be stopped as it hinders progress and doesn't yield positive outcomes. You can live a much more productive life if you think that the present comes because the future exists, and the past derives from the present. As compared with the future exists because of the past. What is important here is what you want to be in the future. This is termed as *your future-self*. Your future-self should be repeatedly imprinting to your brain.

Picture an image of escalator steps descending from above. The steps are coming down from the future toward where you are standing now. If you are unfamiliar with this concept of time flow, try to visualize it repeatedly in your mind. This practice will help liberate you from the constraints of the *standard of time*.

For example, you can start to think in this way:

- I failed before, so I'll fail again. ➡ I'll do better this time.
- I failed the entrance exam for college, so my life is ruined. ➡ My failure on the college entrance exam has nothing to do with my life right now. Let's set a new goal.
- Growing up with parents who constantly denied me from an early age has led me to perceive myself negatively. ➡ My parents didn't give me any affirmation, but that doesn't matter as it relates to my goals.

Using this process, your negative thoughts will be overwritten by positive ones.

## Comparing yourself to others is meaningless

The final thought process that limits efficacy is the *standard of others*. Serious-honor-type students generally think that they must have a certain way according to the *standard of others*. However, if you compare yourself with other people, your efficacy will be lowered.

For example, people who are bound by the standard of others will think:

- Other people can do it, but I can't.
- I am afraid to speak up for myself.
- I must wear the latest fashion.

And so on. They compare themselves to others in every way, and each time they do so, they hurt themselves. However, remember the definition of the ability to believe in oneself: self-evaluation of one's own abilities. The reference point is to compare oneself to no one, and self-assessment is not influenced by others. It is completely up to you.

The above assumption also can be overridden as in these examples:

- Other people can do it, but I can't. ➡ The goals of other people and myself are different in the first place. I should go forward toward my goal, my way.
- I am afraid to speak up for myself. ➡ It's less stressful to speak what I think rather than holding off on what I want to say.
- I must wear the latest fashion. ➡ I should wear what I want to wear.

You can strengthen the power to believe in yourself by eliminating the standard of others from the *Subconscious-Me* and learning to think independently with your own mind.

*Money, past-oriented thinking,* and *comparison with others* are the primary factors that hold you back. By reforming these standards, you can instantly enhance the power to believe in yourself.

# 3.

## The one who controls their self-talk controls their life

---

### Self-talk arises 50,000 times a day, that's why it's important

As previously discussed, feedforward can be applied to oneself as well as to others. Feedforward applied to oneself is basically all *self-talk*. This self-talk encompasses the words you speak to yourself, whether consciously or subconsciously, along with the thoughts, images, and feelings that come with into these conversations.

I believe that the person who controls their self-talk also controls their life. Improving your self-talk can help boost your confidence. There are two types of self-talk: one is the *bubble-up self-talk*, and the other is the *imprinting self-talk*.

*Bubble-up self-talk* can be likened to air bubbles, bubbling up from boiling water, continuously surfacing in your mind. Beginning with simple thoughts like "It's morning, I have to get up," and ending with expressions of fatigue "I am exhausted." People engage in self-talk over 50,000 times a day, often subconsciously, even if they don't voice it aloud.

When the receiver is caught up in undesirable *bubble-up self-talk*, the forwarder should use feedforward to help them rephrase and guide them toward adopting a positive-type of imprinting self-talk.

For example, consider the following:

The receiver says, "I've seen this kind of thing happen before. I must not do it."

The forwarder responds, "You really think so? You may be able to work something out this time. What do you think?"

The receiver says, "I'm anxious about going to work (school)."

The forwarder responds, "That's understandable because it's your first time. Let's do you best. You'll be all right."

## Those who are prone to make mistakes should begin by reviewing their self-talk

Even when we are not consciously aware of it, self-talk occurs in our brain playing a significant role in shaping our self-image and comfort zone, and even impacting our performance. When we make a mistake and engage in negative self-talk such as, "I failed again. I'm no good anyway," our performance tends to deteriorate even further. Even in the face of failure, we can review our self-talk and cultivate a habit of creating positive self-talk, by asking ourselves, "What can I do next?"

It is no exaggeration to say that our efficacy is made up of self-talk. When our efficacy is not elevated high enough, we might be overlooking potential goals and opportunities that cross our minds. Subconsciously, we might be assuming,

"There is no way I can achieve that." This hinders us from recognizing and pursuing potential goals beyond our current circumstances. On the other hand, as efficacy increases, such as when encountering a goal beyond the current situation, we might think, "I may have discovered a great goal! Let's set a goal."

Becoming conscious of your self-talk, you may notice that it tends to be negative at times. When that happens, you have the power to override it with positive self-talk. For instance, when something didn't go well, you could say to yourself, "This time I wasn't myself, but next time I'll be like myself and do better."

When you face difficulties, feedforward yourself by asking, "How can I go about achieving that?"

In the same manner, you can feedforward others as well. You would say to the receiver, "This time you didn't act like yourself, but next time be yourself and achieve what you set out to do. What do you think you can do differently next time?" Ask them, "How can you do that?" and repeat this daily.

Despite being informed about the power of positive self-talk, some individuals may still say, "I can't imagine myself being successful at all," or "I don't feel like I can overcome this difficulty." This is because they are establishing a standard based on their past self. Confirm with them that they understand that time flows from the future to the present. By setting goals, they create self-talk that aligns with the future they want to achieve.

# 4.

## Achieving high goals

---

## High goals and the power to believe in yourself are the twin wheels of success

Feedforward is also done within yourself.

When you lack confidence, you can talk to yourself as follows:

Can I do it? (Bubble-up self-talk)
➡ How can I do this? (Feedforward/Imprinting self-talk)
➡ Yes, I can. (Feedforward/Imprinting self-talk)

Or when you run into difficulties, you must go from "I can't," "I'm lonely," "I want to stop," and "I want to go home" (Bubble-up self-talk) to "What am I going to do now?" (Feedforward/Imprinting self-talk). And go from, "I might be able to do it" to "I can do it" and then to "I'm sure I can do it" (Feedforward/Imprinting self-talk). As you feedforward to yourself like this, your self-talk will become, "Okay, I'm going to do it."

A woman sets a goal of "doing business abroad using English." If she experiences thoughts like "I might get homesick" or "I might not be able to learn English," her efficacy is still low. Conversely, if she perceives *doing business overseas using English* as a natural part of her life and believes *she can achieve it*, her efficacy will be at a high level.

*High goals* and *the power to believe in yourself* are like the two wheels of a vehicle moving toward success. When the two are enhanced, you will naturally advance toward the goal.

## How to increase your efficacy

*Self-talk management* is a powerful method to increase efficacy. Individuals with low efficacy often fall into negative self-talk patterns. It is essential for them to transform negative words into positive ones.

As you consistently replace negative words with positive ones, and good self-talk becomes the predominant pattern, your efficacy will naturally increase. Letting go of the self-talk generated in the past and embracing the self-talk that aligns with your goal will elevate your efficacy to such a high level that you can accomplish any dream you desire.

# 5.

# The high efficacy of the forwarder is crucial

## Get rid of negative thinking

As the forwarder, when you feedforward, your efficacy plays an important role. It is because by witnessing others achieving their goals, people can gain the confidence that *they, too, can do it.*

Efficacy is something that individuals have for their own goals, and it is not about comparing oneself to others in terms of size. However, when a forwarder maintains an extremely high level of efficacy for their own goals, the receiver can also learn how to approach their own goals with a higher efficacy. This is because the receiver's subconscious mind copies the state of the forwarder.

By receiving guidance from individuals with high efficacy in the right direction, you can eliminate negative thoughts such as *What if I fail?* or *I probably can't do it.* Thus, you become able to take action with confidence.

Furthermore, affirmations are effective for enhancing efficacy. Affirmations are a form of *imprinting self-talk* where you express the image of *the person you want to become* in words. You read them aloud to subconsciously instill them. Reading affirmations (preferably out loud) upon waking in the morning and at bedtime can significantly accelerate the speed of goal realization.

## Examples of Affirmations:

- I have many goals that I truly desire, and I live happily every day experiencing the realization of those goals daily.
- I live every day in good health with my family.
- I am proud of myself because I am highly motivated, improving every day, and achieving my goals one after another!
- I am surrounded by friends I love, and I will live happily ever after!

## Efficacy and goals increase at the same time

The goal and efficacy are like two wheels on opposite sides of the same axle; when the goal rises, so does efficacy, and when efficacy rises, so does the goal. They work in tandem to drive us toward success.

In this book, I introduced the core premise of feedforward thinking to be shifting from the current comfort zone to the desired comfort zone. Then, I subsequently explained about the relationship between goal and efficacy. However, setting goals, transitioning comfort zones, and increasing efficacy happen simultaneously.

When the woman, mentioned earlier in the book, set her goal to speak English fluently in Switzerland, her efficacy had already increased at that moment. While sitting next to a foreigner in a café in Geneva, a man asked her to watch his luggage. When he spoke, she recognized the words *toilet* and *luggage*, and realized he wanted her to look after his belongings while he went to the restroom. This boosted her confidence in her ability to communicate, and she successfully placed an order from a menu written in French, using her broken English.

As a result of this one experience, her efficacy increased, and she began to think, *I can do it*. At that moment, dopamine was released in her brain, and self-images of learning and later engaging in smooth conversations appeared simultaneously in her mind. Driven by this, she started attending an English school.

A young boy who became passionate about creating

robots was inspired when he learned about what a particular robot creator was doing during his middle school years. This made the boy think, *I can do it too*, and he immediately started aiming for his goal.

# 6.

## Acquiring the power to involve and move people

### The power to involve and move people

As previously discussed, the first power is *the power to see the future* (= goal setting), and the second power is *the power to believe in yourself* (= efficacy). The first and second powers are crucial when explored based on cognitive science. When these two powers are strengthened, you can achieve anything. I hope advanced forwarders will thoroughly understand this and masterfully utilize it.

While it is undoubtedly true that with sufficiently high levels of the first and second powers, you can achieve anything; in practice, you come to realize that setting clear goals and maintaining high efficacy are quite challenging to accomplish.

Therefore, I have developed a new approach that encompasses concepts like "progressing together with fellow members versus alone" and "climbing up to the comfort zone using individuals with elevated efficacies." I refer to this as the third power, *the power to involve and move people* and I am utilizing it.

Do you have anyone around you who, you think, does not possess exceptional abilities themselves, yet they seem to achieve results by being uplifted by those around them? I've asked many people the same question, and it seems that nearly everyone has at least one or two such individuals in their peripherals. Indeed, individuals who advance due to their interpersonal skills are a prime example. There's nothing wrong with this; such individuals possess a strong power to involve and move people (the third power). This allows them to be lifted by those around them as well. Gradually, they find their ability to set goals (the first power) and their efficacy (the second power) also increases.

## Seven Powers and Feedforward

To achieve a goal, proper goal-setting and high efficacy are essential resulting in a shift of the comfort zone. However, as mentioned earlier, goal setting can be challenging. Efficacy levels might not reach the desired height. Therefore, we can use a reverse approach that is to first, shift the comfort zone ahead of time and then, expect to enhance the goal-setting ability and efficacy. For this purpose, the third power, *the power to involve and move people*, comes into play. This one power is divided into seven powers. Each of these seven powers has *Feedforward Thinking* as its foundation.

1. **The power to encounter: The power to meet the people who live in the goal world you are striving for.**

   When you establish a goal, and your brain acknowledges that the world of that goal is now within your comfort zone, your *Subconscious-Me* takes charge, advising you on the appropriate places to be, the clothes to put on, the food to eat, and the way to introduce yourself, among other aspects. Feedforward plays a pivotal role in heightening your future awareness, enabling a clearer visualization of your goal world. Engaging with the people who live in the world you envisioned is also a proactive step toward realizing your future aspirations.

   Meeting people in the goal world becomes more challenging as the goal becomes higher. Nevertheless, this practice is quite common among successful individuals.

2. **The power to connect: The power to connect someone you admire to someone you met in your goal world. This power helps you put down roots in the goal world.**

   Upon entering your goal world, you are still beyond your depth. To firmly establish this world as your comfort zone, you must actively contribute, allowing you to find your place within it. If you have a desire to contribute, you'll surely find a way. An especially effective way to do this is to introduce someone you trust and respect to someone who is already a resident of the goal world.

The comfort zone is mainly made up of people, so by introducing remarkable individuals you know to the residents of the goal-world comfort zone, you'll become appreciated. When you introduce someone, you make connections that lead to both parties' futures, and this approach embodies a feedforward thinking perspective. Of course, the fundamental principle of *Feedforward Thinking* is focusing solely on the other person's benefits without consideration to your own.

3. **The power to be trusted: The power to have confidence in what you are doing and what you are saying.**

To gain trust, the key lies in having *the power to believe in yourself*. Sharpen your *Subconscious-Me* to be 100% confident in your words. By wholeheartedly believing in what you say and do and by elevating your *Subconscious-Me* to a point of unwavering certainty, you naturally gain the trust and respect of the residents of the comfort zone associated to your goal world. As you consistently self-administer feedforwarding, your ability to believe in your future will grow stronger.

4. **The power to be recommended: The power to present yourself in a straightforward manner which makes it easy for others to introduce you and recommend you within the goal world.**

   As you gain the trust of those in your comfort zone within the goal world, they may inquire, "How should I introduce you to others?" or "What should I tell people about you?" Having a simple word or *tagline* that describes who you are, and what your abilities are becomes quite useful at this point. Do you have a one-word tag that encapsulates your desired future state and the environment that you envision? The process of creating such a tag starts with feedforward thinking: What do I want to be?

5. **The power to communicate: The power to effectively communicate your thoughts at the level of your and the other's *Subconscious-Me* through sharpening the power to see the future and the power to believe in yourself**

   Once you've built a strong relationship, utilize feed-forward thinking to discuss your goal. When your *Subconscious-Me* truly believes that the goal world is your comfort zone, it will naturally communicate your direction to the other person's *Subconscious-Me*. It's important to strengthen your *power to see the future* and your *power to believe in yourself*.

6. **The power to implant: The power to convey information gradually without imposing it, so that the other person can decide for themselves.**

It becomes important to convey your thoughts in words so that the other person can consciously understand you. However, it's essential not to force your message onto theirs. When information is imposed forcefully, even if it's a good idea, their *Subconscious-Me* will resist. Instead, it's preferable to intentionally reveal information piece by piece and leave some blanks. By doing so, the listener's *Subconscious-Me* will naturally organize the information, filling in the gaps. Consequently, they will eventually perceive your initial message as their own idea. Think about your own communication style, while remembering to share information gradually without any push. When you deliver the information to people by feedforward into the future, it reaches them more deeply and steadily.

7. **Power to nurture: The power to remind others so that the information conveyed is not forgotten by them.**

Once you've planted the seeds and seedlings of your goals, don't forget to nurture them with care by providing water, fertilizer, and vigilant oversight. If you don't remind them regularly, they easily forget who you are and what your dreams are. There are several ways to achieve this: in-person, via phone, letter, email, or through social media and networking platforms. The communication during this process should always be feedforward. Such reminders will become positive through feedforward.

As you consistently remind others of your aspirations, the people around you will naturally step in to support you in various ways, like saying, "I can introduce you to someone with more knowledge about what you want to do," or "I have information that might be helpful to you."

# CLOSING

Thank you for reading this book to the end.

As of the date of publication it has been more than ten years since I determined to spread and establish *Feedforward Thinking* in the world. I was convinced that by doing so, many people would be able to achieve amazing results and truly feel happy. As I mentioned in this book, a significant turning point for me was when I witnessed a family member's illness healed with feedforwarding method.

After achieving mastery of *Feedforward* on my own, I spent three years preparing myself for entrepreneurship and starting up my own business. I then launched a company which continues to grow presently. Since the early days of my business, many people have supported me. My understanding and skills have evolved as I have achieved successes. I am a professional coach, and my business is a coaching company. Of the various techniques of coaching, the one I have been using the most is feedforward.

I have been using methodologies such as *goal setting, affirmations*, and *self-talk management*, but what I have used the most often and most effectively is *Feedforward*. In essence, the entire concept of coaching can be found in

*Feedforward*. In fact, a single phrase of feedforward, "What do you want to do now on?" contains the concepts of *goal-setting*, *efficacy*, *self-talk*, and *affirmation*. Upon this realization, I was taken aback and couldn't help but exclaim, "Wow!"

Feedforward is a profoundly simple method, and anyone can use it. Also, it has a contagious effect on those who experience feedforward to become interested in learning more about it. Seeing the successful results of feedforward often entices people to give it a try themselves. The key principle is to *think from the future*.

Feedforward has a positive impact on both you and people around you. It is common to start feedforwarding to someone other than yourself. Then, an attitude of future-oriented thinking is developed in their mind. Interestingly enough, when you feedforward to someone else, feedforward thinking also takes root in you at the same time.

Once the operating system of *Feedforward Thinking* is launched within you, you naturally become attuned to the future and driven to work toward it. Thus, you become a person who has a goal-oriented mindset, and your transformation process begins to unfold.

In Chapter 1, I shared the story about a businessman who won the new-business competition through feedforwarding. During the first half way of his journey toward this success, he received my feedforward sessions. As the sessions progressed, he gained his confidence to independently manage the situation on his own.

In another case, there was a woman who was worrying if she should marry or pursue her career. While I was feed-forwarding, she made a spontaneous choice as indicated by saying, "I'm getting married and going to Hawaii." She promptly acted upon her decision and got married to her husband of Hawaiian descent. They raised their child for a year or two in Hawaii. Then, together with her husband, she returned to Japan. Prior to her return, she was saying, "We are moving to Japan because we want to live in a more exciting environment." With her own feedforward thinking, her comfort zone was continuously being updated.

The power of *Feedforward Thinking* lies in acquiring the future-oriented mindset and the questioning and dialoguing skills, which can be self-administered. Your internal conversations sound something like the ones below.

- What do I want to do next?
- That's right. What can I do with that then?
- That's good. Let's do it.

Engaging yourself in this process of questioning and dialoguing guides you toward your goals. Once feedforward thinking and the necessary skills are acquired, they can be applied throughout your life. Being mindful of the future and actively working toward it can profoundly transform your life and the lives of those around you.

# EPILOGUE

Five years have passed since I wrote, *Itsumo Kekkawodasu Bukanisodateru Feedforward* (Feedforward to Develop Subordinates who Always Produce Results) published by Forest Publishing Co., Ltd., 2018 and started activities to promote *Feedforward Thinking* in Japan. It has been extremely gratifying for me to see that Japanese companies, educational institutions, sports teams, and other organizations have adopted the concept of feedforward, and many people are starting to live their lives with an eye toward the future.

*Gifting Feedforward Thinking to the Children of the World* has been one of my most cherished visions, and it is my great pleasure to have many people join me and engage in the feedforward activities moving toward that goal. *Feedforward Thinking* is now available in English. It is my sincere hope that the concept of feedforward, which is steadily gaining popularity in Japan, will reach many readers in English-speaking countries.

My heartfelt gratitude goes to Noriko Hosoyamada, president of PCS Inc, for publishing this book and to Ellie Rie Shollenberger for her translation of the book from the original Japanese into English. Ellie has been an enthusiastic supporter of Gold Vision and Feedforward. I am grateful for her eagerness to translate this book. Also, l would like to acknowledge Bob Quinn, Laurie Regan, and George Trachilis for their great contributions to editing the book, as well as Bobbi Benson for polishing the book into the format that you have in your hand. My appreciation also goes to all the clients, friends, and business partners who support me continually. Without all their help, this book would not have been materialized.

Finally, I would like to dedicate this book to my beloved wife, Seiko and our 10-year-old son, Sho, whose future we look forward to. I am always thankful to them.

It is my sincere hope that this simple concept of *Feedforward* will contribute to countless people's happiness in the world.

*November 2023, Kazuyoshi Hisano*

# Appendix

_____

## Examples of Feedforward Practice Dialog

Here are some examples of feedforward. You can use it not only with the person you want to feedforward (the receiver), but also with yourself.

**To those who express anxiety and worry**
"I wonder if I'll do well in my presentations (exams, presentations, speeches, etc.)."
➡ "You're nervous, huh? How can you calm down?"
➡ "What can you do to prepare?"

**To those who are disappointed or discouraged**
"Aaah, I've lost."
➡ "I'm sorry to hear that."
➡ Respond after a while (depending on the content and situation, the duration can be hours, days, weeks, or months), "What do you want to do next?"

**To those who express a feeling of failure**
"I failed!"
➡ "It's alright! Never mind! What's next?"
➡ "These setbacks can make our life interesting, can't they?"

**To those who are angry or resentful**

"What the hell is that driver thinking! Cutting in!" (while driving)

➡ "That's not safe. Let's just focus on our safe driving."

"What the hell?! Come at me, dude!" (on a train, station platform, street, etc.)

➡ "That's pretty rude. Anyway, what's our next plan?"

## Examples of Consultation
## Careers

### Scenario 1

"I have been consistently performing well in my role and attaining satisfactory outcomes, yet I have not been promoted for reasons unknown. Furthermore, some of my junior colleagues have been promoted ahead of me. I am concerned about how to secure a promotion and whether I will continue to be over-looked. Is there a future for me in this job?"

"Certainly, there are times when you're achieving results, but things might not go exactly as planned. It's about how you want to live from now on, right? Have you figured out to some extent what you want to do in the future? Let's focus on what you want to do and what you can do moving forward."

## Scenario 2

"I am confident that we women are doing the same or better work and achieving the same or better results as the men in the company. We are inevitably at a disadvantage. We have invisible gender discrimination, the burden of housework and child-rearing, and physical disadvantages. I want to take care of both work and family, but I just don't have enough time or energy. I always feel trapped, so I always take it out on my family and subordinates, and it makes me feel guilty."

"Indeed, there are still challenges for women. It's impressive to see you thriving and excelling despite that. What is it that you truly want to do from here on out? I believe you have a lot more potential, so why not take some time to think about what you want to do moving forward?"

## Entrepreneurship

## Scenario 3

"I have always wanted to start my own business someday, but I have not been able to make up my mind and now I am advancing in age. Of course, I would like to take on the challenge even now, but it is difficult to take the plunge when I think of the risks involved."

"I think that's the way it is. What do you really want to do? I think you can do anything, including starting a business, as long as you are properly prepared. Do you want to do it even if it takes some time? Of course, as is often said, if your goal is to simply start a business, it will not work, so it is important to know what you want to do after you've started."

## Management: Distressed Managers

### Scenario 4

1. I have a subordinate with low motivation and am having trouble dealing with him.

2. I am having trouble knowing how to deal with my older subordinates.

3. I have a subordinate who is motivated, but his ability is not improving, and I am wondering what to do about it.

Advice for managers/administrators/leaders with subordinates

"Having even one subordinate is a challenge."

It is important to do the following things:
1. Wish your subordinates to grow and succeed.

2. Listen to them carefully.

3. Feedforward to them in such a way that they can look toward the future, which will lead them to naturally grow.

The same is true for older subordinates. Of course, it is very important to build a relationship of trust as a foundation.

## Specific concerns

1. "I have a subordinate with low motivation and am having trouble dealing with him."

   a. If the individual is aware of his/her lack of motivation
   
   ➡ Adjust the goal setting/target setting and you'll be fine in no time.
   "Which direction do you really want to go?
   "Is there anything I can do to help with that?"

   b. If the individual is not aware of his/her lack of motivation
   
   ➡ That state has become the comfort zone, so shaking up their comfort zone is the key to change.
   "Have you noticed that you appear to be on a stable and predictable path? What do you envision for your future if you continue in this current state? To break free from the status quo, let's introduce something new, something we don't usually try. Let's give the familiar routine a little shake-up and embrace new opportunities."

2. "I am having trouble knowing how to deal with my older subordinates."

➡ Express your appreciation and also express your sincere wishes for the person's success.

"Thank you for everything. I would like to think about what I can do to help you be active in the future, so please tell me the direction you are aiming for."

3. "I have a subordinate who is motivated, but his ability is not improving, and I am wondering what to do about it."

➡ After making them aware of their low skill level, discuss how they can improve their abilities.

"Your passion is great. Now let's work on your skills."

"How would you like to develop your skills?"

## 20-40 year-old (*Yutori*/millennial generation)

### Scenario 5

Tendencies of this generation:

- Less materialistic desires
- Weaker desire for power
- Aversion to competition
- Easily influenced by information
- Aversion to failure

**When giving feedforward**

1. Know one's current position. Encourage them to focus on reality, as there is a tendency to overestimate.

2. Expand the capacity to think about the future, one step at a time, with an eye toward the future through feedforward.

3. Also, teach them the importance of thinking from the goals, and help them to gradually develop bigger goals.

"First of all, I would like you to think about what you want to do. Let's call this your 'destination,' and next, check where you are. We'll call that your 'current position.' The gap between your current position and your destination generates energy. So you need to know where your current position is and then to figure out what you want to do while looking as far into the future as possible. It's good to think about what you can do about that right now."

## Comparison with friends

### Scenario 6

"I have a friend from school who appears to be excelling in both work and her personal life. I genuinely wish the best for her, but when I see her from time to time, I can't help but notice the contrast between her achievements and mine, and it tends to make me feel down. Additionally, I find myself occasionally saying mean things to her, and I feel even worse. When I think the gap between us will get bigger, I can feel impatient and sometimes even like giving up."

"I've been in similar situations where I've felt rushed and anxious. I've also noticed my own mean tendencies and felt down about it. Anyway, putting that aside, what do you want to do from now on? Since worrying about the other person doesn't seem to help much, why don't you start thinking about what you can do on your own?"

## Loneliness

### Scenario 7

A woman moves to a new place, quits her job, and is raising her children. She doesn't know many people yet and doesn't have anyone she can talk to about her problems, so she has to deal with them alone. Her husband is too busy with work and doesn't listen to her much.

"That does sound lonely. In that situation, I think I would also feel anxious. What would make you feel at ease? Maybe you'd like to talk to your husband about it, or have a friend you can casually chat with, or perhaps you're interested in pursuing a job. There are various ways to approach it. Why not start thinking about what would make you happy?"

## Family

### Scenario 8

"I am worried about my mother who is old and lives

alone, apart from me. She does not want to come here to live with me because she is attached to where she lives. My wife (husband) is also not keen on the idea of living with her (his) parents, so we usually end up fighting when this topic comes up. I don't know if I can keep my current job. I hardly get any salary increases, and I have many worries about the future."

"I see. You are worried about your mother. What do you really want to do? What does your mother really want? How about your spouse's thoughts? Let's move forward slowly with this process and think about what would be best."

## Children's education

**Scenario 9**

"My child doesn't seem to enjoy studying, and hardly sits at the desk when at home. Naturally, his grades aren't that great. I understand that academics aren't the only important thing, and I want to support him in wholeheartedly pursuing things he can do right now. However, I also want to ensure he won't have regrets in the future. At least for myself, I sometimes wish I had studied a bit more, and I think it would have been nice if my parents had encouraged me to study. What should I do in this situation?"

"First, I believe it's important to consider what you want for his future and how you want to support your child. It's also crucial to help children develop the ability to think about what they want to do in the future. Supporting and nurturing their *ability to see the future* is essential. There might be things that your child might not see on his own. Both parents can provide support to help him cultivate this ability."

# Glossary

---

**Axis of Greatness:** The axis of setting goals outside the status quo. Chapter 5.

**Axis of Many:** The axis of setting goals in all aspects of your life. Chapter 5.

**Axis of Wanting-to:** The axis of setting goals for something you truly want to do. Chapter 5.

**Balance Wheel:** A circular diagram created to be aware of having multiple goals in each aspect of your life. Chapter 5

**Cognitive science:** A discipline that seeks to explore how the brain perceives and processes information. It is in close proximity to psychology, functional brain science, analytic philosophy, and artificial intelligence research. Chapters 3 and 4.

**Comfort zone:** A state of being familiar to ourselves. It is derived from the English word "comfort" but does not necessarily mean comfortable. It refers to a state that is familiar to our brain. It includes not only physical but also informational spaces. We can demonstrate our skills the best when we are in our comfort zone. Chapter 5.

**Comfort zone sickness:** A disruption triggered by the subconscious mind. It occurs when we are making consistent strides toward achieving an effective goal that we have set. Our subconscious mind acts on us making the goal seem insignificant despite our desire to realize it, creating reasons for us to give up on the goal, and making us feel unwell or causing discord with those who are around us. Chapter 5.

**Conscious-Me:** The source of thoughts and judgments that are in our consciousness and that we can consciously control. Chapter 5.

**Dream killer:** An entity that tries to prevent the realization of a goal. The biggest dream killer can be ourselves. Our family members and other people around us can also become dream killers. Chapter 5.

**Efficacy:** Self-assessment of our own ability to achieve our goal. The degree to which we believe in ourselves--that we can do it. Chapter 6.

**Feedforward:** A technique to encourage people, who tend to be preoccupied with the past and the current situation, to shift their focus to their future and take action to move forward. It begins with communication and observation to understand and accept the receivers' situation and their feelings that are associated with what's happening to them. Chapters 1 - 6.

**Feedforward Action (FFA) process:** A future-oriented decision/ action making process. It begins with setting a goal through feedforward and initiates idea generation for necessary actions to achieve the goal. Simultaneously, it triggers "subconscious reflection" which then leads to "resetting a goal" and "modifying actions." In mid-to long-term FFA, Feedforward includes goal setting and subconscious reflection. In short-term FFA, Feedforward includes target-setting and subconscious adjustment. Chapter 2.

**Feedforward interviews:** Personal interviews where feedforward is carried out. Conducted between supervisor and subordinate, teacher and student, etc. Chapter 2.

**Feedforward meeting:** Meetings conducted with a feedforward mindset. Participants actively feedforward to produce new ideas and to find positive solutions to existing problems. By bringing subconscious reflection and subconscious adjustment to the level of consciousness, it is possible to generate specific solutions. Chapter 2.

**Feedforward session:** The setting in which feedforwarding takes place. Chapter 5.

**Feedforward thinking:** A way of thinking that we can create more value by looking to the future and working toward that future, rather than looking back at the past. Chapter 6.

**Feedforwarder/Forwarder:** The person who feedforwards. Chapter 3.

**Futuristic thinking:** A way of thinking to view that time flows from the future. In this way of thinking, we make a decision on our future first. We understand that as time flows from the future to the present, the decision becomes reality. Chapters 3 and 5.

**Goal:** What an individual or organization aims for. A destination. Chapter 5.

**Gold Vision (GV):** A term made by combining the words "GOLD VISION" and "GOALED VISION." The concept is that if we can set a goal (gold vision) that feels as if it has already been realized, it will be realized. It requires the power to see the future, the power to believe in yourself, and the power to involve and move people. Chapter 5.

**Gold Vision Method:** A system of specific methodologies for implementing the Gold Vision. Chapter 5.

**Have-to:** What we think that we have to or should do, despite not really wanting to. Such a state of mind. Chapter 2.

**Homeostasis:** An innate function or characteristic of the body to maintain physical and mental conditions within a certain range. For example, sweating or shivering to maintain a constant body temperature. Gold Vision views that the concept of homeostasis extends not only to the physical space, but also to the information space. Chapter 5.

**Information space:** The world/space that exists in each person's brain and mind, created by the brain's processing of information collected by the five senses. Chapter 5.

**Level of Abstraction:** The extent of information that defines a concept, under the assumption that there is a hierarchy of concepts. Roughly, it refers to the degree of abstraction. It can also be called the elevation of one's point of view to see things. Chapter 4.

**One-on-one:** Interviews/meetings conducted on a one-on-one basis. Chapter 3.

**Physical space:** The world/space that can be experienced with all five senses. Chapter 5.

**Power to be recommended:** The ability to represent yourself in simple expressions that can be easily summarized and advocated for in the goal world. Chapter 6.

**Power to be trusted:** The ability to have confidence in what you do and say. Chapter 6.

**Power to communicate:** The ability to communicate at the level of subconscious minds through sharpened "power to see your future" and "power to believe in yourself." Chapter 6.

**Power to connect:** The ability to connect someone else to those who are in your desired goal world and to put down your roots in that world. Chapter 6.

**Power to encounter:** The ability to meet the residents of your desired goal. Chapter 6.

**Power to nurture:** The ability to remind others of the information you have given them so that they do not forget it. Chapter 6.

**Power to plant:** The ability to convey information gradually, without imposing it, so that others can make their own decisions. Chapter 6.

**RAS (reticular activating system):** A mechanism in the brain that acts as a filter to selectively determine what information to bring to the conscious mind and what information to keep subconscious from the large amount of information to which we are constantly exposed. Chapters 2 and 5.

**Receiver:** The individual who receives feedforward. Chapter 3.

**Scotoma:** This is a psychological blind spot. A state of being unrecognizable by the RAS due to low importance. Chapter 5.

**Self-esteem:** A self-assessment of one's worth. Self-evaluation established by past accomplishments, such as a self-evaluation of one's current position. Chapter 6.

**Self-image:** The conscious and subconscious perception of one's identity. This concept includes efficacy and self-esteem. Chapter 6.

**Self-talk:** Language that we speak to ourselves. Images recalled along with the language are also included and treated as self-talk. Chapter 6.

**Self-talk, bubble-up type:** Self-talk that comes from our subconscious. It includes not only words, but also images and feelings. Chapter 6.

**Self-talk, imprinting type:** Words that we consciously speak to ourselves in an attempt to influence our subconscious mind. Chapter 6.

**Sense of reality:** The feeling as if you are actually in that space. Chapters 3 and 5.

**Standard of money:** An (undesirable) value and way of thinking that money holds absolute value. Chapter 6.

**Standard of other people:** An (undesirable) value and way of thinking that determines our own evaluation based on other people's evaluations. Chapter 6.

**Standard of time:** An (undesirable) value and way of thinking that sees time as flowing from the past and views the future as an extension of the past and present. Chapter 6.

**Subconscious:** This refers to everything except that which we perceive with our conscious mind. Chapters 5 and 6.

**Subconscious-Me:** The self that is almost impossible to control consciously, making its own thoughts and judgments that are difficult/impossible to recognize because they dwell in our subconscious. Chapter 6.

**Targets Short-term goals:** Specific things to be accomplished. Chapter 2.

**The first power:** *Power to see the future:* The ability to have a Gold Vision and feel a sense of reality in the goal world. Chapter 6.

**The second power:** *Power to believe in yourself:* The ability to truly believe "I can do it" (Efficacy). Chapter 6.

**The third power:** *Power to involve and move people:* The ability to gain trust and support from the other people and the ability to have them resonate with our Gold Vision. Chapter 6.

**Visualization:** Imaging and visualizing. In feedforward, visualization includes information from the five senses (sight, sound, smell, taste, and touch). Chapter 6.

**Want-to:** What one truly wants to do, or the state of wanting to do it. Chapter 5.

# About the Author

Kazuyoshi Hisano is the president of Conoway Inc., a company specialized in coaching organizations and individuals who want to grow without limits.

He is the founder of Gold Vision University and Feedforward Online Salon. *Feedforward Thinking* is widely accepted and implemented in many organizations in Japan. More than 500,000 people are currently practicing feedforward thinking. He also teaches Coaching programs at Temple University Japan.

He is the author of *CEO Coaching: How to Grow Without Limits!* and *Gold Vision: See Your Future, Believe in Yourself, Involve and Move People* which are available in English.

### Official Sites:

http:/ /kazuyoshi-hisano.net

http://conoway-inc.com